Mountain Biking
Pocket Guide

The Mountain Biking Pocket Guide

Clive Forth

FALCON GUIDES

GUILFORD, CONNECTICUT
HELENA, MONTANA

AN IMPRINT OF GLOBE PEQUOT PRESS

Cover photograph © Frazer Waller
Inside photographs © Frazer Waller
Illustrations by Tom Croft
Commissioned by Charlotte Croft
Edited by Becky Senior and Sarah Cole

This book is produced using paper that is made from wood grown in
managed, sustainable forests. It is natural, renewable and recyclable.
The logging and manufacturing processes conform to the environmental
regulations of the country of origin.

Designed and typeset by Susan McIntire in
8.5 on 11pt Helvetica Neue Light

Printed and bound in China by C&C Offset Printing Co.

Library of Congress Cataloging-in-Publication data is available on file.

ISBN 978-0-7627-7998-7

10 9 8 7 6 5 4 3 2 1

Note
While every effort has been made to ensure that the content of this book
is as technically accurate and as sound as possible, neither the author nor
the publishers can accept responsibility for any injury or loss sustained as
a result of the use of this material.

Contents

Acknowledgments

Thanks to Vicky and Bob, my late parents, who gave me the freedom to dig jumps in the garden, R.I.P.

Thanks to my brother Kevin, whose ace bikes were a major contributing factor in me finding my purpose in life.

To John, Adam and Vanessa, R.I.P.

Thanks to Beeg, Jockey, Ian, Steve, Walker, Fev, Willie Howard, Woody, Rob Lee, Gav, Pip, Jan, Mike W, Mike T, Charlie, Robbie, Jamie, Craig, Tally, Wendy, Jemma, Big Mark, Mark H, Big Dave, Wendy, Rory and Duncan; special thanks to Sam and Lyndsey from Bike Village for the support.

Thanks to Frazer for his wonderful images, and to Sean, Graeme, Mary and all the staff at Surf Sales, Transition Bikes and Dakine. Thanks to Dave Price and Dr. Yu for keeping my body in check. Thanks to the crew at The Shed in Mabie Forest for your continued support, and thanks to Scotby Cycles.

Last but not least, thanks to Charlotte Croft, Becky Senior, Naomi Webb and all the staff at Bloomsbury for their sterling work, and thanks to all of you out there who love riding trails.

Clive Forth
www.mtbskills.co.uk

Foreword

It was about 1990 when I first heard of Clive Forth. In those days I was riding a duck-egg blue Raleigh Memphis – I believe they were made in a Russian gulag out of iron and Communists. It rode like a plow and I felt like the ox trying to pull it (most bikes were like that back then). My friend, John, kept saying, 'Come and ride with Clive this weekend, he's mental!'

Well, I met Clive on a standard autumn Saturday afternoon at the local woods. Margaret Thatcher was still running Great Britain and the conversation soon turned to politics – although clearly Clive was much more focused on his bike. 'What angle have you got your brake levers at?' he asked out of nowhere. I was puzzled, what did this have to do with poll tax riots? 'Oh it's just you need to angle them so that they're at a similar angle to your arms.' You see, Clive loves the details – get the details right and the rest follows. He can not only tell you where to place your bike on every corner he's ever ridden, but also what angle your hands should be on the bars, or why you don't need to brake into that particular corner, or even how many bottles you should take into the shower.

Since those early days, we have been riding and talking bikes ever since. We moved on from domestic politics and drove around the country entering every mountain-bike race we could afford while discussing the finer points of bicycle evolution. Mountain biking back then was in its infancy; the bikes still wouldn't hold up for long without something breaking. On any given ride you would generally hear something like, 'Did anyone bring an adjustable wrench?' or 'You go on without me, I think I'll have to walk home…' Clive wasn't bothered though – for him, this just added to the challenge. And he would always be the one trying a new crazy method of getting from A to B! Of course, we would all then give it a try. More often than not, this would end in a trip to the hospital or worse (a trip to the bike shop!).

We tried every form of mountain biking on these old contraptions and should be congratulated for sticking with it in the dark days before sealed bearings and full suspension! But as the bikes became more capable, so did Clive. I remember when disc brakes became a worthwhile investment; from this point on, following Clive became extremely dangerous. He just kept riding the front wheel! Down a steep bank, through a gate, on his dad's bed… One minute you would be flying down a hill, the next thing you know, Clive is in front, back wheel in the air and you are about to have a face full of Panaracer Smoke tire! Years later, while riding with him in the Alps, the reason behind all that nose-wheelie practice became clear: lots of tight switchbacks that most people couldn't even walk down and what do you know? Clive nose-wheelies smoothly into the corner while swinging the back wheel out, drops into the switchback and he's away.

For a long time, Clive has been the personal skills trainer to me and many of our friends. We have spent 20 years following Clive, watching what he does, copying his lines, trying to capture the moment as he does it. He has turned us all into skilled bikers and we thank him for that. During this time, Clive has also turned himself into a skilled teacher. I have to say though: this book does worry me! I've actually become quite good at mountain biking, and I like that. By following the tips and tricks in this book, there will be many more accomplished bikers on the trails, so please, whatever you do, ignore everything you read in this book. It's nonsense!

Before I go, I would just like to ask Clive one final question: when are we riding next?

Barry Gell
Rider and friend

Introduction

Most children like bikes, though some more so than others. I was surrounded by engineering in my youth, from large industrial plant machinery to finely tuned racing cars, and this had a profound effect on how I looked at my bike and the possibilities of riding. My early bikes were hand-me-downs from my older brother Kevin. Growing up through the late 70s and early 80s and having an older brother meant I got to ride some cult classics, from the Striker onto the Grifter, then the legendary Burner. The Chopper eluded me, but a neighbor did have one so I got to savor its terrible handling on the odd occasion.

There was one bike though which defined what it was that I loved about riding: the Bomber, Raleigh's mass-production klunker. All my early bikes had an upright riding position, which lent itself to motocross-style riding and drifting turns, but the Bomber's larger wheels and chunky tires made for a whole new era in goofing around on dirt. Those early play days in the garden, around the streets and up in the woods opened up a wonderful world to me.

I have been on a great many journeys with my friends since I started racing mountain bikes in the late 80s. Over those years I've ridden thousands of miles and had relatively few incidents, and fortunately I have been with quick-thinking friends or trained professionals at events when I've been injured (something we refer to as a 'bio-mechanical'). And thanks to my early years and my inquisitive nature when it came to mechanical failures on the bike, I had the tools and ability to keep on riding – few rides resulted in me being stranded and unable to finish. In this book you will find hints and tips on how to prepare for a ride, look after yourself and others while out on the trails, improve your key riding techniques and get more from your mountain bike experience. I have had a great time dissecting the key elements that make for a great rider, and I hope they bring you closer to the essence of mountain biking.

1 Pre-ride

Mountain biking is more than just a leisure activity or sport – for many it is a way of life. More and more people are taking to the hills to ride trails. When I started riding mountain bikes back in the 80s there was little outside influence; other than the occasional feature in the emerging American magazines, there were no real reference points. My early adventures with like-minded friends would take us away from our urban surroundings and out into the hills, where our days were spent searching for that all-important flowing single track. Having prepared a route on our map over a cup of tea, we would pack our bags and bikes with the essentials for the day and hit the road.

Equipment back then was less capable than it is today, and we often had to deal with mechanical failures, also called 'mechanicals' and the occasional injury which we called 'bio-mechanicals'. My friends and I soon became very capable at fixing most common problems and breakages; we also developed a high level of skill when it came to riding the bikes and an ability to navigate using a map and compass. I now take these skills for granted, so in this book I want to share that knowledge and help you to improve your mountain bike experience. The most important thing to remember is that poor planning has the potential to develop into poor performance and, in the worst cases, expense and/or injury!

▶▶ Tip

Checking your equipment should be done in advance, preferably the day or night before.

So before we head out onto the trail it is important to make sure we have the correct equipment for the task, and that it is well maintained and in good working order. When planning a ride you should also take into account the following points.

Weather conditions

Weather in mountainous regions (in fact, pretty much anywhere you're likely to ride) can change very quickly, so always be prepared. Carry spares for your bike and extra clothing, including a wind- and waterproof jacket. You may be riding a trail that is relatively close to a population center, but do not be complacent; a rider who has crashed could go into shock, and your extra clothing layers could be vital in keeping them warm enough while waiting for help.

Most weather reports on TV and radio are very basic and do not contain specific information for the region where you will be riding. There are numerous websites for weather prediction, and most hostels and resorts have phone numbers where you can check regional weather and get the most accurate and up-to-date predictions – just remember that even the professionals get it wrong from time to time!

Go online for up-to-date and in-depth information.

Trail conditions

Trails can change as weather and riders erode them; a trail may ride completely differently from one day to the next. Weather plays a huge part in how a trail will ride: dry, hard-pack trails ride much faster than wet, muddy ones. A wet trail will sap more energy and you will also have to lower your speeds when riding technical sections – your average speed will drop accordingly. So, when riding in adverse conditions, allow extra time to complete your ride. The terrain, weather possibilities and distance of your ride will dictate what you should be carrying alongside your basic equipment. On shorter rides, basic provisions such as first aid kit, spare inner tube, patch kit, pump and multi-tool would suffice. If the weather is poor then of course you will need to take your waterproof gear. On longer rides you may want to add some spares and food.

Trail ratings

Different countries (and, sometimes, even regions within those countries) have different systems for grading trails and so unfortunately you may find inconsistencies. The length, elevation, gradient/inclination, width, exposure and technicality/surface (see page 15 for an explanation of these terms) are usually taken into consideration when trails are rated, and most places employ the color-code system used for ski runs. Remember though that the rating of a trail would have been set by a designer/builder who may have a different opinion than you or me regarding what makes a trail more technically challenging – you should bear in mind that any rating is a rough guide only, and expect that sections on the trail will challenge you and push into the next grade up.

Decide what sort/level of trail you want to ride. Do you have the right bike and associated safety equipment such as knee, shin and elbow pads? Is the trail within your and your group's capabilities?

Navigation

Mountain biking has its inherent dangers; it just wouldn't be the same without them. You may come across another rider who

Color codes for ratings

Green = easy family trails, mainly on wide open track with small hills and easy gradients.

Blue = slightly narrower than green trails, longer in distance and may include technical trail features and purpose-built single-track sections.

Red = technical trail features and increased elevation, gradient and exposure will be common on red grade trails; these trails are aimed at the real enthusiast.

Black = exposed trails with longer distances, lots of technical trail features and steep gradients; aimed at riders with a high level of ability.

Double Black Diamond = signifies bike parks, jump spots, etc.; NorthShore 'raised timber' trails are common features on these most difficult trails. Aimed at highly experienced and ambitious riders.

Ride within your limits and obey all signage.

Quick guide to terms

Elevation: Height gained and lost.

Gradient: How steep the trail is.

Inclination: The way in which the gradient is measured, usually in % terms.

Width: How wide the trail is.

Exposure: How exposed to the elements and to potential danger if you go/went off the trail.

needs your assistance, or it could be you or a member of your group that needs assistance – so get to know the area before beginning the ride. Most bike parks and resorts have trail maps. Some trail maps only provide a rough guide to the layout of the trail network and surrounding landscape. You should always back up a poor map with a proper one.

When navigating a non-marked ride, you should know if the trails allow mountain bikes to use them. Different parts of the world have different laws and rules regarding trail use; you should work in harmony with the authorities and respect the rules. Riding trails is a privilege, not a right.

▶▶ Tip

Before you set out, check if there are points in the route at which you could 'short cut' if feeling fatigued or in need of assistance. You may find yourself having to cut a ride short for one reason or another, and having a good understanding of the surrounding area could save a life.

▶▶ Tip

When navigating a ride, cut out an area of the map just larger than the area that you intend to ride in, seal it in a clear plastic bag, and keep it in an easily accessible pocket.

Topographic maps show exhaustive detail of the features on the ground, allowing you to pinpoint your location easily – for more information, take a look at www.omnimap.com, which sells a large selection of maps for pretty much anywhere you can ride around the world.

Work from left to right to find the longitude.

Then work up the scale to find the latitude.

In the United States, topographic/USGS maps use a grid reference system that breaks the landscape down into degrees, minutes, and seconds and also into square miles.

How to find a GPS reference

A GPS reference is a series of numbers, the first half of which is your latitude, the second your longitude. The longitude gives you a vertical line on the map that shows where you are along the east-west axis. The latitude gives you a horizontal line across the map that tells you how far you are along the north-south axis. Where these two lines intersect, that is your location.

Navigating with a GPS

The Global Positioning System is a navigation system that uses signals from Department of Defense satellites to determine the map coordinates of a GPS receiver by triangulation. The use of mobile GPS units has become more commonplace among bicyclists, and several types of handlebar-mounted cycle computers now

As I grew older my rides became longer and my inquisitive nature meant that I was eager to discover new trails and link them, creating a single track for the ultimate ride. I used to keep a diary to help me remember rides, and hours were spent drawing on maps and testing trails. For me this is an intrinsic part of mountain biking, discovering hidden valleys and woods while appreciating the landscape from many aspects.

feature a GPS function in addition to the familiar odometer/speed-ometer functions. These computers use the rider's GPS-determined coordinates to calculate distance traveled. The calculations are not constant, so a GPS-based odometer won't be quite as accurate as a well-calibrated device with a spoke-mounted magnet.

Most GPS use among cyclists is casual, even recreational. Perhaps the most popular feature of this high-tech wizardry is that it allows a rider to upload their GPS information onto a computer and view a three-dimensional map of the day's route with elevation gain.

Communication

Where are the nearest points of communication in the event of an emergency? Carry a mobile phone that is fully charged and turned off (and even if the phone has no credit, you can still call emergency services), but remember you may be out in an area that has no signal, so do not rely on this alone. Satellite phones (or 'satphones') offer better coverage but still have limitations, and are also quite expensive compared to normal mobile phones.

There are also a multitude of satellite tracking devices which have emergency call buttons; when pressed, these send a signal for emergency services to locate you. When carrying such devices, ensure that the batteries are fully charged and that you know how the system functions.

Time

How long do you expect the route to take? Always have a contingency plan in place, leave details of your route with a family member or friend, and make sure someone knows where you are going and when you intend to be back. You should factor in any stops you will make and allow a bit of extra time for any potential mechanical issues.

Spares and supplies

It is essential to be hydrated and nourished before going out on a ride – riding on an empty stomach will deplete your body of essential vitamins, minerals and nutrients. You should definitely take something to eat and drink on most rides, as you never know how long you may be out (a string of mechanical issues could result in you being away from civilization for much longer than you had anticipated). So, what spare equipment should you take?

Notes from the trail

Eager to ride big hills one winter, we made a long drive in search of some remote wilderness. Equipped with everything we needed for a day in the hills, we set out on another intrepid adventure. However, a string of mechanicals and deteriorating weather got the better of me: sweat cooled on my skin and the high winds on an open ridge drained me, my core temperature dropped and hypothermia was setting in. Vitally, no one in the group panicked, level heads were kept and we navigated a shortcut back down out of the wind. Later, the seriousness of the situation dawned on me when my friends told me how bad I looked. Never underestimate the mountains!

Tailor your kit to suit your ride, but always remember the must-haves.

Packing your backpack

- *First-aid kit* – I highly recommend the inclusion of super glue for sealing small cuts (it was developed for this purpose in the Second World War); tampons for plugging large bullet-type wounds (which can be created by brake levers and branches); a mouthpiece for cardiopulmonary resuscitation (CPR); water-proof paper and pencil to record notes—for example, the times if the casualty becomes unconscious; and rubber gloves for your personal protection.
- *Fluid* – water and/or sports drinks. The average amount in all weather conditions is approximately 750ml per hour.
- *Maps* – back up copied maps with a more detailed topographic map.
- *Multi-tool* (see glossary for description) – including chain breaker, Torx head keys, Allen keys (i.e., for star pattern and hexagonal headed bolts) and screwdriver.
- *Tire levers* – some tire/rim combinations may require levers (good-quality plastic ones are light yet robust and won't damage aluminum rims).
- *Spare inner tubes* – make sure you have the correct valve (I carry Presta valve inner tubes as they fit all common rim styles).
- *Puncture repair kit* – adhesive patches are easy and quick to use as they do not require glue.
- *Tire patch* – an old plastic toothpaste tube is ideal; remember that you will need a knife or scissors to cut it to the appropriate size for the tear in a tire.
- *Tubeless tire patch kit*.

- *Duct tape* – this can be used to hold a tire patch in place (instead of packing an entire roll, wind a length of tape onto a plastic card).
- *Pump* – choose a good-quality pump (my personal favorite is the Topeak Mountain Morph). Try to avoid storing this on the bike as it will be exposed to the elements, which may impede its performance. Look after your tools and they will look after you!
- *Spare derailleur hanger* – this is a piece of aluminum that bolts onto the frame – most bikes now have replaceable hangers. They act as a fail-safe, bending or breaking as opposed to damaging the main frame.
- *Quick links, replacement chain link* – make sure you get the correct link for your drivetrain, e.g., Gold = 9 speed, Silver = 8 speed.
- *Spoke wrench* – to fit your spoke nipples (the part that is inserted through the rim and screws onto the spoke); there are various types, so make sure you're equipped with the correct tool.
- *Specialist tools and spares for your particular bike* (this could be anything from shock bushings to hydraulic brake components; tailor your kit to suit the location and type of ride you are taking on).
- *Mobile phone* – charged up, with credit and switched off; it's advisable to store this in a waterproof container or bag.
- *Wind- and waterproof jacket* – lightweight garments are preferential as they pack down into a small bag and will fit into your backpack with ease, though on summer days and in hotter climates a lighter alternative outer layer may be more appropriate.

Above: Replacement chain link.
Left: The derailleur hanger.

Some of the items you need in your kit: tubeless repair kit, spare pedal set, replacement spokes, cables, a tire patch and an empty toothpaste tube.

You should tailor your equipment to suit your ride. On longer rides and in bad weather, pack more food and suitable layers, and in warmer climates pack sunscreen and extra fluids. Optional additions for longer rides in more remote terrain include:

- *Multi-tool* – with cutting implements, small adjustable wrench or pliers.
- *A mixture of bolts, nuts and washers* – you can take these from old or worn-out components (these are best stored in a waterproof container or bag).
- *High-pressure shock-absorber pump* and/or a replacement shock pump.
- *CO_2 canisters and inflator* – these make for a quick fix (fast tire inflation from a compressed gas cartridge eliminates wasting energy using a traditional pump). Be careful though, as the canister cools when it expels the gas, so you should wear gloves.
- *Electrical in-line connector* – for repairing a broken gear or brake cable (screw the connector onto the cable and re-join it).
- *Gear cable* – make sure it's a longer rear gear cable (which also works on a front derailleur).
- *Zip ties* – these can be used to attach a gear or brake cable to your frame. They can even be used in emergencies to hold various broken components together.

- *Replaceable spokes* – these will only work with traditional hub and rim systems.
- *Replacement for broken pedal axle* – a carriage bolt with two washers and nut makes for a quick fix.
- *Brake cable* – for those of you using cable-operated brakes.

Bike preparation

Now that your pack is equipped, you have time to tinker with the bike. If you need to change your tires, do it in the comfort of your shed or garage rather than in a windswept parking lot. These tasks consume energy, and the more you can save by working in a dry, warm environment the more you will have for the ride. In an ideal situation, things like changing tires or lubricating the chain, sprockets and suspension pivots should be done the day or night before.

Tires

Tire choice is extremely important. You should match the tire to the terrain and conditions. Large tires with a deep tread will perform well in certain conditions but less favorably in others. There are many variables to take into account, and you will always be compromising one way or another when selecting a tire, but they are a critical component that can dramatically change the performance and feel of the bike, so serious consideration should be taken when making your choice.

Tires are sold by diameter and width (both measured in inches), and by compound. Most mountain bikes have 26-inch diameter wheels, but 29-inch wheels are becoming more popular; 24-inch wheels are quite rare. Tire widths range from 1.5 to 2.5 inches: different manufacturers produce slightly different sizes, but the most common measurements you will find are 1.5, 1.75, 2.0, 2.2, 2.35 and 2.5 inches. There will be lots of options in the cut of the tire: the cut creates the pattern or tread of a tire and can range from large oblong blocks to small knobs. The cut of tires can make a huge difference to ride quality and grip. There are various rubber compounds used for tires, and manufacturers sometimes create their own names; ask your retailer what the options are.

The tire's sidewall may be folding, in which case Kevlar strands have been used to create the casing and bead (the part of the tire that locks onto the wheel rim), whereas traditional tires are made with a wire bead. These are heavier but more robust than folding Kevlar tires, and there has been a trend over the last decade to produce various sidewalls that are stiffer and less prone to being cut.

Larger tires

Heavier tires (2+ inches in width) offer better rim protection and a smoother ride, with a greater cushioning effect. The larger contact area gives improved feel and better traction. The likelihood of pinch flatting (i.e., when the tire is compressed and the inner tube becomes pinched between the squashed tire and wheel rim, puncturing the tube) is reduced, especially when combined with the thicker sidewall casing. However, larger tires have a greater rolling resistance (due to the extra mass). Larger, tougher tires are the best choice when riding in areas with a lot of sharp rocks.

Smaller tires

If your ride involves a substantial distance on roads, then you may want to opt for a smaller, lighter tire with less rolling resistance. Remember though that you will have less traction and that smaller tires are more prone to pinch flats, cuts from braking and gashed sidewalls.

If you have not completed many rides, and have not yet developed a sixth sense for terrain and prevailing conditions, talk to other riders for information on tire choice. There are a multitude of Internet forums (see page 126) all teeming with folk who want to share their knowledge and opinions.

The following is a guide to help you choose the right tire for different conditions. You will need at least two different sets of tires for the opposite extremes, depending on where you live and what you ride. For those of you riding skate parks and streets, a low-profile tire will suit all your needs.

DRY	DRY/DAMP

Semi-slick: Use when trails are dusty, loose, rocky and hard-packed. Look for small side blocks that are close together, with a center ridge or low-profile knobby pattern and a rounded profile. Fast-rolling tire with good traction in the turns, though braking and accelerating becomes compromised due to the smoother contact area.

Medium-size knobby: Larger blocks, still closely packed, give more grip in all directions and are still relatively fast rolling. Consider a slightly harder compound or higher pressure if you want to decrease rolling resistance. Traction on smooth surfaces will be reduced when running higher pressures and harder compounds.

Low-profile knobby: Similar to a semi-slick but without the center ridge. Small, evenly spaced blocks give a consistent feel on all surfaces and are fast rolling with better traction for acceleration and braking. The rounded profile is more suited to using on the rear (rounded profile tires on the front have less bite when turning in and crossing cambers).

The large, flat edge blocks might fill with soil and fine dust, so in these conditions look for a tire with a split block so the mud can shed when the tire deforms.

▶▶ Tips

- Try and choose a tire that is tailored to suit the larger percentage of surface you will be riding on.

- When conditions are wet and the soil is sticky and heavy, especially in clay, then a small, narrow and spiky tire will give exceptional traction for driving, braking and cornering. The narrow profile will also give ample mud clearance.

INTERMEDIATE/WET	WET
Large square or oblong blocks with large spacing. Some tires will have split blocks to help with clearing mud. More grip can be achieved on hard surfaces using softer pressures and compounds. The larger blocks will give a bigger footprint and more adhesion.	Tall spiked blocks with large spacing for mud clearance. A narrower tire may be preferential when riding in thick clay-like mud. Be wary about using deep aggressive cuts when riding on rock and woodwork (the cut of a tire is its tread pattern – some tires have taller blocks and others smaller ones).

TYPE	PROS	CONS
Large tire Deep tread, 2.2–2.5"	• Better traction • Added suspension	• Increased rolling resistance • Heavy
Medium tire Medium tread, 2.0–2.2"	• Good traction • Slight suspension	• Less grip
Narrow tire Low tread, 1.5–1.8"	• Fast rolling • Lightweight	• Less grip • Hard to fit • Thin sidewall vulnerable to pinch punctures

And what about street tires?

- Slick – small cut
- Semi-slick – medium-size blocks, rounded profile

Slick street tires.

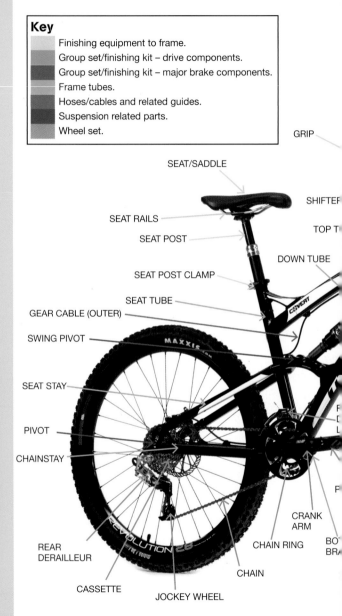

Key

Finishing equipment to frame.
Group set/finishing kit – drive components.
Group set/finishing kit – major brake components.
Frame tubes.
Hoses/cables and related guides.
Suspension related parts.
Wheel set.

GRIP

SEAT/SADDLE

SHIFTER

SEAT RAILS

TOP TUBE

SEAT POST

DOWN TUBE

SEAT POST CLAMP

SEAT TUBE

GEAR CABLE (OUTER)

SWING PIVOT

SEAT STAY

PIVOT

CHAINSTAY

CRANK
ARM

REAR
DERAILLEUR

CHAIN RING

BOTTOM
BRA

CASSETTE

JOCKEY WHEEL

CHAIN

Anatomy of a mountain bike

STEM

HANDLEBAR

HEADSET

BRAKE LEVER

HEAD TUBE

BRAKE HOSE

FORK STANCHIONS

TIRE

BRAZE ON/
CABLE GUIDE

SHOCK
ABSORBER

WHEEL RIM

DISC ROTOR

SPOKE

BRAKE CALIPER

VALVE

Pre-ride inspection

Before you hit the trail, it is important to make sure that your bike is in good working order. Clean and inspect it. A mountain bike is exposed to lots of little bumps and shocks which are absorbed into all the components and, over time, these may break or work loose. Mountain bikes are also exposed to the elements; water, muck and grime will work their way into components, particularly the moving ones, and this will wear them over time. Remember, look after your equipment and it will look after you!

So, don't be shy here – grab things, shake things and have a good visual inspection of your equipment. Tighten or adjust accordingly. Should you find a component that is excessively worn, attend to it before you hit the trail.

1. Make sure your wheels are tight. Check that the lever is properly closed (it should leave an imprint on the skin of your palm when closed). Try not to over-tighten though, as this will stress the metal and stretch the threads, reducing effectiveness.

2. The lever on your front wheel should point either upward or rearward. Avoid closing it against the fork leg, as you will not be

Check for brake pad wear and ensure that your wheels are fixed securely.

able to get a good grip on it should you need to undo it. This is particularly important in cold weather. Bolt-through systems (i.e., large oversized axles held in with pinch bolts or similar) need to be checked also; once again, avoid over-tightening the small Allen bolts, as they are likely to sheer or pull the soft aluminum thread out of the fork stanchion.

3. Your rear quick-release (QR) lever should point rearward and upward; you can angle it into the rear triangle, but make sure you can get a good clean grip on it. Never have it pointing downward (it could hit rocks and would be moved in the direction that loosens it).

4. Check your seat quick-release to make sure it is not going to injure you if you crash: it should be tight enough so the post does not drop or move around easily (but avoid over-tightening it).

5. Now grab the saddle and try to rotate it, then move it up and down by holding the nose and tail, in order to ensure that it's not loose on its clamp. Make sure there are no rips or splits in the saddle and that the rails (i.e., the metal frame) are not bent.

6. Grab your bars and try to twist them. If they move, it could either be that your grips are moving or that the stem bolts need

QRs take a knock from time to time.

tightening (again, do not over-tighten). When tightening stem bolts, work on opposite sides, tightening the diagonal ones first. Make sure the gap between the clamps is even all the way around.

7. Now grab your brake and gear levers and see if they are tight. I recommend that the brake levers are set so that they move in a crash (i.e., tight but not too tight), as this could save you and the lever blade from injury and breakage!

8. Stand in front of your bike and grip the front wheel between your thighs. Now try and move the bars clockwise and counter-clockwise. Hopefully the stem does not spin around – if it does, tighten the clamp bolts onto the fork steerer (the tube that comes up from the front forks through the main frame). Make sure you tighten a little at a time on the bolts, and keep the gap between the main part of the stem and the clamping part even.

9. Below the stem is the headset. Check that it is tight and there is no play in the bearings. Lift the front wheel in the air and turn the bars/wheel left and right; if it is tight, then the bearings are under too much load or are excessively worn. If there is a tight spot,

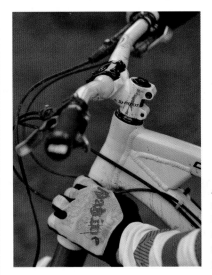

Any movement in an oversized headset will be felt where the fork enters the head tube of the main frame.

then you have a bent steerer tube on your forks. The movement should be quiet and easy. A rough-feeling and noisy headset is either worn out or needs lubrication (which can't be done at trail side), so if in doubt get your local bike shop to take a look.

10. Now place the wheel on the floor and stand behind the bars. Apply the front brake and rock the bike backward and forward. While you are doing this, place your hand around the top bearing race and feel for play – if you can feel movement then the headset is loose. Repeat the process with the lower race. On modern bikes you may feel a slight movement from either the fork stanchions or the brake pad moving in your disc brake caliper. To help eliminate this, turn the wheel to 90 degrees and rock the bike without using the brake. You could also rest the front wheel against a wall and rock the frame.

11. If you have not just changed them, check your tires for pressure and wear – make sure that the knobs/blocks are not peeling away and that there are no bulges or rips in the sidewalls.

12. Lift your front wheel and give it a spin, then look and listen. A wheel that does not spin freely will slow you on the trail and

Check that the spokes are tight and do not have excessive play. Image on the opposite page shows how to check an oversized headset for play (felt in the bottom race).

cause you to use more energy than is necessary. If it does not spin freely, your hub could be worn or over-tightened (you will need to adjust the hub or replace the bearings) or your brakes could be binding (if using rim brakes, you may have a brake pad rubbing, in which case adjust them so that they allow the wheel to spin). If you are using disc brakes and the wheel does not spin, the disc rotor may be bent, in which case it will either need straightening or replacing. Alternatively, you may have sticking pistons in the brake caliper and the brake may need bleeding. These are definitely jobs for the bike shop!

13. Grab the tire and rock the wheel left to right – if there is movement, either the quick release is loose (you should have checked this and therefore eliminated this possibility already, see page 28, point 1) or more likely the hub is worn and/or loose. Run your hand around the spokes, plucking them to make sure none are loose. Take a good look at the rims to make sure there are no dents or cracks – check thoroughly and look for buckles and flat spots.

14. Repeat the previous two steps with the rear wheel, remembering to spin it in the direction of travel (forward) so that it will freewheel.

15. Spin your cranks around, rock them from side to side, make sure they spin freely and have no play.

16. Spin your pedals around, make sure they spin freely and have no play.

17. Do a visual inspection of brake hoses and gear cables and ensure that there are no splits or leaks in hydraulic systems and no splits or frays in cable outers and inners. Look closely, as these often split near the shifter, derailleur or where they pass pivots on full suspension bikes.

18. Examine the brake pads carefully. On bikes equipped with rim brakes, you need to make sure that the brake pad is not rubbing on the tire or going to miss the rim and hit the spokes – make sure the whole pad contacts the rim. For bikes with disc brakes, take a good look at pad wear and the condition of your brake rotors. Make sure there are no leaks and the rotor is straight and firmly secured onto the hub.

Make sure all areas that have bearings spin freely and have no play.

19. Check your drive system (see diagram on pages 26–27; drive system components are marked with green arrows) for wear and lubricate your chain if necessary, but use sparingly. Avoid using non-specific lubricants as they are often too viscous and attract dirt to the chain, increasing the rate of wear. Use a Teflon-based spray lubricant on your derailleur and a specific spray lube for fork stanchions and shock absorbers – be careful not to get any on your brake rotors as this would make the brakes ineffective and could result in loss of control. If you do, clean them with brake disc cleaner. Wet weather riding will eat into components much faster than dry weather riding, and keeping your drive system free of dirt will increase its longevity and make that winter ride a more enjoyable experience. Worn drive components should be replaced to avoid damage to other components in the drivetrain system.

20. Check that your gears are working and that you can move the shifter easily and smoothly. You should replace your gear cables on a regular basis to ensure a light and concise shift (the definition of 'regular' depends on the rider – obviously if you ride 20 miles every day of the week, you will be replacing parts more often than

Holding the main frame, try and move the rear end to feel for play in the pivots and bushings.

someone who goes out for a 10-mile ride on the weekend). To lubricate the cables: select the largest sprocket at the back and, without pedaling the bike, shift down to the smallest sprocket; this will give you lots of slack cable, and you can unhook the cable through the slots in the braze-ons (the part on the frame that the cable slots into) and slide the outer, allowing access to those covered-up sections. Clean the cable, apply some grease, and fit the cables back into the braze-ons.

21. Suspension units should be checked for leaks around the dust seals and adjusters; on shock-absorber systems which use air as opposed to coil springs, check the pressure at regular intervals. Move the back end of the bike around to check for loose pivots and swing links; tighten and/or replace if necessary. I personally recommend upgrading original shock mounts with harder-wearing precision versions.

►► Fuel in my backpack

Personally, I take a few cereal bars, a banana and some energy gels (which are high in carbohydrates and digest easily). These travel well in my biking backpack, which has a section with a bladder capable of holding a few liters of water and a drinking tube. This gives me easy access to fluid on the move and saves fumbling around with a water bottle (most bottles will only hold 750ml so are only good for short rides or on rides where I know I can refill).

The bag is packed and the bike is ready! If you have not done so already, eat a good meal which is high in protein and carbohydrates, and get a good night's sleep. Before setting out on any ride you should eat breakfast (or lunch/dinner for later starts) and while on a ride you should eat little and often, to avoid excess energy being consumed in digestion.

Time to hit the trails?

Not quite. Before we put ourselves through the rigors of riding off-road, we should limber up. Mountain biking requires us to move in a very dynamic fashion and stretching before and after exercise can radically reduce the risk of injury. Cold muscles are tense and need to be warmed and relaxed in order to function properly; a cold muscular system can easily be injured or lead to damage to the skeletal system (tight muscles can pull bones in undesired directions). There are specific methods, with numerous books and classes available, to help: yoga, Pilates and tai chi can help train your body when not on your bike, but some basic stretches will help to keep you supple when not in class. See the back of the book for some resources that can guide you through these essential warm-up exercises.

2 Trail etiquette

Basic etiquette

While you are out on the trails, be it a wilderness ride or one in a local park, you may come across other riders and different trail users. It is important to remember that the countryside is there for everyone's enjoyment, not just us mountain bikers. I'm sure you wouldn't want anyone to spoil your day out, or put you and your friends in danger, so please ride responsibly and treat other riders and trail users with respect.

Mountain bikes that are ridden in a controlled manner are generally quite quiet and have little impact on the environment, which means it is very easy to startle walkers, horses and their riders, and wildlife. When approaching other trail users, you should slow down and greet them politely with a 'hello' or 'good morning/good afternoon'. Take your time to pass them and give plenty of space where possible. On very tight single-track trails, it may be advisable to stop and stand off the trail. This may not be possible in all situations, for example steep gradients – loose surfaces and rough terrain can make it very hard to slow down. I have been in a good few of these situations myself and it's not nice – this is one rare instance where the pedestrian should yield to the mountain biker.

In general, you should control your speed and only let your pace build where good sight lines allow. When riding in a group, give each other plenty of space so you can spot your line; needless changes in pace can cause bottlenecks, and a section that could be ridden with ease becomes a walk.

▶▶ Tips

If you are riding with a possibility of adverse weather or poor light, avoid wearing dark colors and put some lights on your bike.

Also, always remember to check beforehand that the trail you are using allows mountain bikes.

Riding in primative areas

The International Mountain Biking Association (IMBA) has carried out extensive studies on the environmental impact of mountain biking, and has come to the conclusion that bikes ridden in the correct manner cause less erosion than most other trail users, and because we pass wildlife in a swift and silent manner, we generally therefore cause little disturbance to it.

You should try to avoid skidding where possible and stick to the trail as best you can; this is especially true when riding in primative areas. Bad weather conditions can accelerate trail erosion, so if you know that a particular section of trail holds a lot of water then try and avoid it. The trail will soon get cut up and the ride line will become wider, encroaching into the surrounding vegetation. The end result? A nasty scar on the landscape and a trail section that becomes unridable.

Depending on the route you have chosen, there may be a need to ride on, or cross, public highways; it is essential that you familiarize yourself with the rules and regulations in the particular area you are in. Highways are a way to link sections of trail and therefore make longer routes, but an off-road alternative is still preferable.

Notes from the trail

Mountain biking is a medium that has taught me many lessons. Whether you ride solo or with a bunch of friends, mountain biking is a personal thing. With each ride comes a new experience, a new challenge and a new lease on life. Maybe you rode a climb you would normally push your bike up, or you made it smoothly through that off-camber root section. Or maybe you broke your bike beyond trailside repair and had to walk home. Whatever happens, look for the positive, focus on the process, reflect and progress.

▶▶ Tip

There are call signs which indicate that a faster rider is approaching and wishes to pass: 'rider!' or 'rider up!'. I have also heard 'track!' or just plain 'left!' and 'right!' called out. Always give plenty of notice if you are the faster rider, and if you are the slower rider make plenty of room as soon as you can. If you are the faster rider, be patient and wait for a good space before you attempt to overtake – a rash decision could result in an unnecessary accident.

Purpose-built trails

Bike parks are getting more numerous as mountain biking increases in popularity. These purpose-built facilities have specific trails of varying difficulty with neat signage and on-site facilities such as bike rental and refreshments. When you're riding at a place like this, a faster rider may catch up with you or you may catch up with a slower rider. As you would with other trail users in the wilderness, control your speed and greet them with a polite 'hello'.

Trailside manners

At some point in a ride it may be necessary to stop – your bike might need fixing or you may just want a break for something to eat or drink and to appreciate the view. When stopping during a ride, make sure you stand well off the trail and ride line, remove your bike from the trail and avoid laying it down with the gears facing the ground, as this risks damaging them (think 'gears to the sky'). It has happened to me on a few occasions that, after rounding a blind turn, I see riders and their bikes strewn all across the trail. You wouldn't park your car in the middle of a main road, would you? Fortunately, so far, I have been able to respond in time and so avoid a nasty collision. It is important to remember that we are all out on the trail for similar reasons, and no one wants a premature end to their enjoyment.

▶▶ Trail etiquette

- Ride in a responsible manner.
- Give way to other trail users.
- Be polite and courteous.
- Respect the rules of the road.
- Avoid skidding.
- Stick to the trail as best you can.
- Give way to faster riders as soon as you can, and do not intimidate slower riders.
- Stand off the trail when resting or working on your bike.
- Take your trash with you.

Make sure you stand off the ride line.

When carrying out repairs at the trailside, take your time. Be methodical in your approach, and take care to not lose items in long grass. Always take your old inner tubes and parts with you and leave no trace of having been there. Some fruits, banana peels for example, can take a long time to decompose, so take all litter with you. This still applies, of course, if you are on a purpose-built trail. Remember that every hour that rangers spend picking up litter is an hour less spent on building or maintaining the trails.

Common sense, common safety

Obey all signage. Familiarize yourself with the symbols and key on the map, and do not under any circumstances enter areas marked 'DANGER!' These areas could be firing ranges or hunting zones; there may be un-detonated explosives on the ground; quarries could be using explosives; or there may be unstable cliff faces. Foresting operations will involve heavy machinery and should also be avoided. Read the signs, follow detours, and keep an eye on what's around you and where you are on the map.

3 Trailside repairs

Despite the improvements made to mountain bike technology over recent years, nothing is infallible. At some point you may have an issue with your bike. When you stop to investigate and (hopefully) repair your bike, combinations of weather conditions can create unfavorable circumstances. Wet, windy days and cool temperatures are all that is needed to open up the potential for a dose of hypothermia. Sweat cools on the skin and body temperature drops rapidly in these situations; I speak from experience, and I would not wish it on anyone.

Even in a bike park scenario, we must be prepared and capable of dealing with mechanicals and bio-mechanicals; a broken chain can easily be mended and a long walk therefore avoided. There are some components that, with a bit of ingenuity, can be 'repaired.' (I say that in the loosest sense of the word!) Whatever you repair may not perform to its original level, but at least you can ride out.

Mechanicals

Familiarize yourself with your equipment. It is particularly important that you get to know how your wheel clamping system works. Most bikes have a variation of the standard quick release (QR) lever, where you undo the lever and loosen the nut slightly to remove the wheel. Some modern forks and rear ends have bolt-through systems, which all differ slightly, so make sure you know how your system works. You may need to carry tools; the multi-tool covers most Allen bolts, but as some bikes still have nut and bolt set-ups it is really important to know which applies to you.

▶▶ Tip

There are many ways in which we can 'park' our bikes on the trailside while stopping for refreshments or to carry out repairs. Each has its own merits and disadvantages. For example, in order to deal with one of the most common problems we encounter, the classic puncture, if possible I prefer to put my bike upside down on a soft surface to remove the wheel.

Method 1

With the bike upside down, you remove the possibility of damaging components and therefore protect the high-value areas of your bike (rear dropouts, fork leg lowers/dials/dropouts, rear derailleur, chains and chainrings will all be out of harm's way). Laying the bike down on its side puts weight on the rear derailleur, which will decrease its longevity (its small pivots have not been designed to deal with a load in this position).

Method 2

You need to find an area that is large enough to stand your bike up and that lets you move around it safely. The worst that can happen if your bike is upside down on a rough surface is a tear in your seat, and even this is unlikely. You may get a scratch or two on the brake/gear levers, though this is purely aesthetic and will not detract from performance.

Some jobs, like adjusting a headset, will require you to keep the bike upright. When stopping to rest, lean your bike against a wall, tree or similar solid feature, or lay it down but ensure that the gears are facing the sky.

Fixing a puncture/changing the inner tube/ fixing a tubeless tire

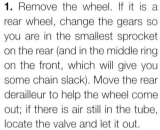

1. Remove the wheel. If it is a rear wheel, change the gears so you are in the smallest sprocket on the rear (and in the middle ring on the front, which will give you some chain slack). Move the rear derailleur to help the wheel come out; if there is air still in the tube, locate the valve and let it out.

Above and left: Swing the rear derailleur up to help the axle pass when removing the rear wheel.

2. Start at the valve by pushing it in through the rim slightly. Pinch the tire, so that the bead pushes into the deeper section in the middle of the wheel rim.

Let all remaining air out of the tire.

3. Work your hands down and away from you, pinching thumb against forefinger and gathering all the bead into the center of the rim. This will give you plenty of slack on the other side to roll the tire off with your palms or, if needed, to insert a tire lever. When using levers, try and roll the tire bead off the rim as you lever it out. You can try sliding the lever along if there is some slack.

There are some exceptions to the easy-to-fix puncture. Downhill rims, tubeless tires and various combinations of tire and rim can be awkward, in which case you may need to use tire levers.

4. Remove the tube. If you know for sure that it is an impact puncture, then either swap the tube or inflate it to see where the two telltale slits are, in which case move on to step 6.

5. Inspect the tire. If you have a slow leak, it could have been caused by something like a thorn, a piece of wire or similar sharp object. Be careful – any object that is sharp enough to puncture your tire will be strong enough to puncture your skin. For this reason, I don't advise running your hand around the inside of the tire to find a puncture; instead you should pump the tube up, feel (with your hand just above the tube surface) and listen for escaping air, and look for the hole. Line the valve up with the rim and tire so you can easily locate the approximate area that the foreign body is in.

6. Remove the object using your multi-tool to assist, then patch or replace the tube.

If you have a slit in the tire, patch it with your old toothpaste tube and some duct tape. For tubeless tires, poke in a small piece of tire patch before inserting sealant and re-installing.

A fast patch makes a fast fix – no glue, no mess.

7. Next, put the valve into the rim and tuck the tube into the tire. Start at the valve and work either side of it, pushing the tire over the lip of the rim using your thumbs. Hopefully you'll have enough slack when you get to the opposite side of the valve to just 'pop' the tire on the rim. Some combinations may need levering on, in which case be careful not to pinch the tube.

8. Pull the valve down and replace the lock ring where applicable (Presta valves are my preference, as they are thin and have a metal lock ring to keep the valve exposed).

9. Now inflate, taking your time so as not to damage the valve by thrashing around with the pump. When using CO_2 canisters to inflate, be aware that they get very cold as the gas is released, so wear your gloves.

You should end up being able to pop the tire on by hand.

Line the chain up with the smallest sprocket when re-inserting the wheel.

With the wheel firmly seated in the dropout, tighten the QR.

10. Replace the wheel, ensuring that the QR is tight and out of harm's way.

Mending a broken chain

Chains break for a number of reasons: it could be excessively worn, you may have caught it on a rock, or there could just be a weak link.

1. Drop the front and rear derailleur into the smallest chainring and sprocket combination, as this will give you lots of slack to work with.

2. Find the bent links, or if the chain has broken you will need to untangle it and remove a link or two.

3. Use your chain tool/chain breaker to remove any broken/bent links.

4. If you do not have a quick link or replacement pin, you can use the existing pin; it does however create a weaker joint.

5. Feed the chain back through the drive system.

6. Re-join the chain with a quick link or joining pin.

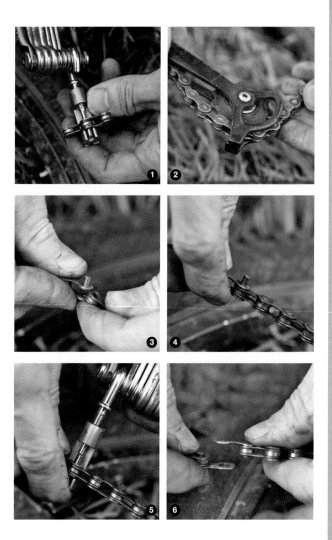

7. Be aware that a shorter chain may not be long enough for you to select certain gears. Avoid putting excessive strain on the chain and rear derailleur by not using combinations of large chainring and large rear sprocket.

With the chain on the big chainring and small sprocket, the jockey wheels (2 small sprockets on the derailleur) should sit vertically.

Adjusting gears

Cables stretch over time and your indexing (the amount of movement allowed by the shifter indent) may wander, leaving you with skipping and jumping gears. Most systems will have a barrel adjuster (or two) located somewhere that will enable you to remove the slack from the inner gear cable and re-align/index your gears. Your gears may also not function smoothly if the chain, chainring or sprockets are excessively worn.

1. Make sure that the rear derailleur is not bent by sighting it from behind.

2. Either get someone to hold the rear wheel off the floor by holding the seat (mind those pedals!) or turn your bike upside down. Turn the cranks around and shift into the middle chainring and small sprocket.

3. Check to see if the stop screws are set correctly by lining up the top jockey wheel with the smallest sprocket. Look from behind or above the bike.

Make sure that the derailleur and hanger are straight by sighting from behind with the bike upright; everything should sit on the vertical.

The jockey wheel must line up exactly with the sprocket. If the jockey wheel does not line up perfectly, adjust the stop screw by either turning it:

- clockwise to stop sooner in its movement; or
- counterclockwise to allow the derailleur to move farther.

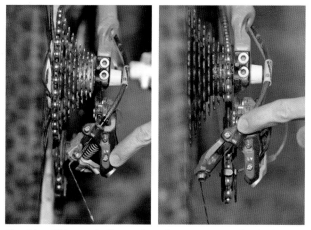

The 'L' on Shimano indicates the adjustment screw for the large sprocket, i.e., low gear.

4. Repeat the alignment process with the jockey wheel and the large sprocket. You can do this by pushing the derailleur up with your hand (until it won't go any farther) while turning the cranks.

On a Shimano derailleur, the top screw is for the lower sprocket and the bottom screw is for the top sprocket, so you should adjust accordingly. On a SRAM derailleur, the screws are marked 'H' and 'L'. 'L' is for the top sprocket and 'H' is for the bottom sprocket.

5. Now check that the B tension screw is set so that the chain can run freely between the top jockey wheel and sprockets. There should be a gap approximately the depth of the chain between them when sighted from the side. By adjusting the screw clockwise you increase the gap and vice versa.

The chain should run freely off the sprocket over the jockey wheel.

SRAM derailleur adjustment screws are located in a different place than Shimanos.

6. To check whether the gears are indexed (and so shifting) properly, shift up and down through the gears while turning the cranks around. Go through each gear one at a time to see if the gears run smoothly – if they do not, move on to step 7 but if they shift OK, then you're all set to carry on with your ride.

7. Starting in the smallest sprocket, shift up one gear at a time. If the chain does not go up to the next sprocket, you need to put more tension into the cable by turning the barrel adjuster counterclockwise. If the chain jumps up more than one sprocket, then the cable is too tight and you need to slacken it by turning the barrel adjuster clockwise. Work the bottom four sprockets; this is where the spring in the derailleur is under the least tension, and if you can get a clean shift between these small sprockets then the rest of the cassette (sprockets) should be fine. If you end up fully winding out the barrel adjuster, you may need to take up extra cable slack by adjusting the cable tension using the cable retention pinch bolt located on the derailleur (see step 8).

If you have a rapid-rise system, which are rare these days, then the reverse of the previous points applies.

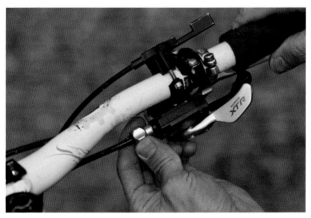

Barrel adjuster located on the shifter.

8. Fully screw in the barrel adjuster clockwise, then unwind it a couple of turns. You should have the chain on the smallest sprocket at this point. Undo the cable pinch bolt on the derailleur and pull the cable through, re-tighten the bolt and repeat steps 6 and 7.

Replacing a derailleur hanger
The rear derailleur hanger is a fail-safe device designed to bend and break, preventing the main rear triangle from being damaged.

1. To replace, undo the rear derailleur and remove from the hanger.

2. Undo the retaining bolts and remove the bent/broken hanger.

3. Replace the hanger with a new one from your pack.

4. Reattach the rear derailleur and check your gears for alignment and indexing as above.

Straightening a bent wheel
Occasionally, wheels will go out of true (that is, they bend and are no longer straight). You may have landed sideways or just taken a few large impacts. There are a couple of neat ways we can true a wheel at the trail side, but ultimately you should get a professional wheel builder to re-true, tension and dish your wheels in a wheel alignment jig. To simply get you out of the woods and back to civilization though, the following pointers should help out.

1. Turn your bike upside down.

2. Place a finger on your frame or fork next to the rim so that it rubs on the rim edge. You can use a zip tie if you have one, though you will need to cut it to length.

3. Position your finger or zip tie so that for the most part you have contact with the rim surface. Slowly, taking care that your finger does not go into the spokes, spin the wheel and watch the rim. Does it move left or right?

4. Spot the bent section and stop the wheel. Check the tension in the spokes and either tighten the spokes on the side that the gap appears or loosen the spokes on the far side from the bend. You may need to do a bit of both in extreme circumstances.

5. You should make small adjustments at either end of the section that is bent and larger adjustment nearer the center. Take your time and make small adjustments, being careful not to put

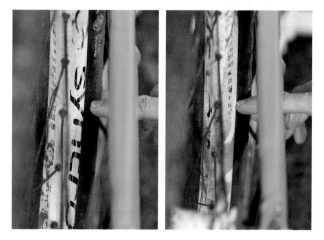

too much tension into the spokes as this may cause a flat spot. Keep checking the gap as you go by feeding the wheel past your finger or zip tie.

If you have buckled the wheel so badly that it won't spin in the frame, then deflate the tire, remove the wheel, and take off the tire and inner tube.

1. Place the wheel on the floor and stand on the rim with one foot, gently applying pressure through the other side (high side) with the other foot. Tough wheels and big bends will require more effort. Avoid jumping on the wheel, as this will excessively weaken an already weakened rim and it may fracture.

2. Hold the hub in your hands and spin the wheel; repeat step 1 if necessary. When you have got it looking less like a potato chip and more like a bike wheel, put it back in the frame or fork and go through the previous 5 steps to make the final adjustments.

Broken spokes

You can either remove them completely, although you may need to remove the disc rotor or cassette to do this. Alternatively, you can bend and wrap them around the other spokes so they do not catch on the frame. Replacement temporary spokes are available and are a handy addition to your pack; they will however only work on traditional spoke and hub combinations.

Wrap the spoke around another spoke or remove it completely.

Fixing a broken gear or brake cable

This is a very uncommon scenario, but worn gear cable housings and frayed inner gear and brake cables can break. Typically, a cable housing will give way near pivots on suspension bikes and up near the shifter where the cable moves when turning the handlebars. The housing breaks and the inner cable then loses tension. If the inner wire breaks, then you can use an electrical in-line connector from your pack to re-join it. If the housing has broken, then the following steps will get you going again.

Rear gear cable

1. Undo the pinch bolt and remove the inner cable.

2. Put the outer casing in your pack.

3. Feed the inner wire through the cable stop on the rear derailleur.

4. Hold the derailleur so that you are in a gear which lets you pedal up hills with ease.

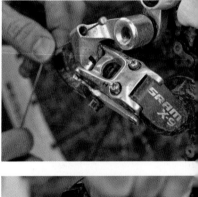

5. Pull the cable tight and lock it in the pinch bolt.

6. Wind the excess cable in a loop and secure with duct tape from your pack. If you have cutters, you can trim the cable.

Front gear cable

1. Place the chain on the middle chainring and hold the derailleur so that the chain does not rub.

2. Adjust the inner stop screws so that the derailleur stays in place. If there is not enough adjustment then either ride in the inner chainring or remove the inner cable and slide it through the last cable stop (braze-on) so that the nipple sits in the braze-on. Adjust the derailleur so that it stays in position over the middle ring and tighten the cable in the pinch bolt.

I use an old set of pedals for my spares when guiding people on rides; the lightweight aluminum body and titanium axles add little weight to my pack.

Fixing a broken pedal

1. Insert a carriage bolt with washers or a replacement axle from your spares kit.

2. If the pedal axle is stuck, then unfortunately it's a sketchy ride or a walk home, as this just cannot be fixed at the trailside.

4 Skills & technique

A mountain bike skill or trick is simply a combination of techniques performed in harmony.

Now that you have the tools of the trade and are capable of using them, it's time to perfect some technical skills on the bike. Trail riding becomes much easier when you know how to perform the key skills and techniques – over time you will learn when to use them to help smooth out that trail and get more from your mountain biking.

Why is it important to practice skills and technique?

When we use good technique, we save energy and cheat the trail by using gravity and momentum to aid our progress. That way, we have more energy in the tank to spend when we need to. Being efficient and smooth allows you to ride farther and faster. Taking hits from the trail by riding into small wheel-sucking holes and bashing into square edges (like rocks and roots) slows your forward progress and burns energy unnecessarily. Ultimately, if you can get your wheels up, onto and over obstacles, you will flow through the trail with relative ease. Get the basics down and see for yourself just how much more your mountain bike experience opens up for you.

Basic core riding skills and techniques

Mountain biking is a skill-based sport and can be learned in a progressive manner in a safe environment. Diversify your riding and try not to be in a hurry to hit the trail each time you ride; instead, set aside some time during your ride to practice, practice, and practice some more. A seemingly boring forest road section can be turned into a playground with a little imagination.

Notes from the trail

As technology improved and components became more robust, my time spent in the workshop decreased. This gave me extra time to play on the bike and develop my core skills. If you can find just a few minutes each day to play on your bike, you will see a rapid improvement in your ability when you get out on the trails. You will also get a good workout in the process, increasing your strength and flexibility. These mini training sessions add up and make all the difference.

SKILL 1: Braking – speed control

Before we operate any piece of machinery, we must familiarize ourselves with its components and the essential parts that stop the machine. For us mountain bikers, that of course means our brakes. Your front brake is the most efficient and, if used correctly, will slow you safely and efficiently.

How to address the brake lever

Moving the brake levers in (i.e., toward the stem) allows you to hook your first finger at the end of the lever blade. By holding the end of the lever you have maximum available leverage, quite literally at your fingertip. The lever blade will go through a longer arc at the end, as opposed to somewhere closer to the pivot. This in turn enables you to have greater/finer control on how much brake you apply (you also remove the potential of crushing your own fingers by not using your index finger). The most efficient part of braking comes from the initial contact that the pad has with the disc (or that the pad has with the rim).

The rear brake is the lever of choice in certain situations, such as crossing wet roots in steep terrain. However, contrary to popular belief, we will not fly over the handlebars if we use our front brake in steep downhill terrain! Always try and keep your wheels rotating, as this will give you added traction and make braking more efficient.

Three fingers on the bar for maximum purchase and one finger for featherweight braking.

For most situations we use both brakes together, making quick and controlled movements on the lever, increasing and decreasing pressure as the trail surface changes beneath our tires. As you descend on a trail, you should be constantly adjusting and balancing your use of the brakes in an effort to maintain a preferential speed.

Braking on different surfaces and on different gradients

Stay centered over the bike. Resist the temptation to move over the rear of the bike; if we drop off the back too far, we hyperextend our limbs and eliminate our ability to steer and lean effectively on the bike. We also remove our mass from above the wheel. When we are too far back, we have nothing more to give if the gradient gets steeper. You will be amazed at how steep an incline you can ride down and still remain centered over the bike. You will not be catapulted over the front as long as you can lift your front wheel up, onto and over obstacles.

Loose surfaces mean constant adjustment of technique, as small rocks on hard surfaces will roll under your wheels. By dipping the heels and wrists we help drive the bike into the ground, forcing

Just breathe and relax, grip will return!

the tires to bite harder. Remember to remain relaxed – being supple is key to letting the bike move around and find traction.

Braking bumps

Braking bumps are a series of ruts in the ground caused by people locking up their wheels when decelerating for a corner, all riding a consistent line, and suspension bikes being set up too hard. Try and ride closer to the edge of the trail on a smooth section; by adjusting your line through a section you can slow down more effectively and will find more grip when cornering. Suspension can be adjusted to compensate for the bumps. You need a faster rebound and compression to deal with the

▶▶ Key points

- Grip the end of the lever using your first finger.
- Pull the lever gently, slowly increasing the pressure.
- Apply both brakes together.
- If you lock a wheel, release the pressure before reapplying the brake.

stuttering effect that braking bumps create. The best option though is adjusting line choice.

SKILL 2: Neutral stance – rolling along the trail

We will refer to the basic riding position as your neutral stance or center. This stance is also sometimes referred to as the attack position or ready position.

You may have read about weight shifts. Try and think of the bike as being the weight, rather than your body – move the bike below you, not your body over the bike. When we shift weight, we are not dramatically throwing ourselves forward on the bike or leaning off the back; instead we are using pressure through the feet and hands to lean the bike, press it into the trail and 'unweight' it in a neutral position – we are aiming to float through the trail when the going gets rough, and gain free speed from the trail where and when it is smooth. This is done in a very subtle manner and only in extreme circumstances do we need to thrust our own mass around to move the bike in a desired direction. Through applying good technique, we remove the need for using brute force.

Avoid sitting when you are coasting down trails. When you are sitting, you become fixed to the bike and will feel each and every feature of the trail. You need to be standing in order to use your limbs as suspension. Remember, we are trying to move the bike around below us while keeping our head and upper body relatively still.

The following points should help you to master an effective neutral stance:

- You will have a favored foot (your lead foot) and the other foot (your trailing foot). Roll along the trail with your lead foot to the front, keeping your cranks level (parallel to the ground). You should have the balls of your feet just slightly in front of the pedal axles.
- Stand up on the pedals and keep your body centered over the bike above the bottom bracket area.

Neutral stance

Practice your neutral stance.

| Keep your body centered over the bike | Look ahead | Avoid putting weight on your hands |

| Stand up on the pedals | Heels dipped | Lead, or favorite, foot to the front | Wrists dipped |

- Try to focus your body mass through your feet onto the pedals and cranks. Avoid putting your weight through your arms and therefore the handlebars.
- Avoid moving too far toward the back, as you will lighten the steering and risk losing control.
- Look ahead, relax and drop your heels, resisting the temptation to lock your limbs out.
- The wrists and heels should also be dipped slightly, ready to absorb any impacts. By doing this we create a fulcrum, so if you hit a square edge then you're forced onto/into the bars and pedals. But if you hit a square edge while riding toe down, your foot might slide off the pedal.

SKILL 3: Selecting the correct gear (shifting)

Constantly changing gear in order to complete a consistent number of revolutions per minute (that is, each revolution of the pedals) will help you to get more from your ride. Riding in too small or large a gear is inefficient and will reduce the distance you're capable of covering.

Reduce the amount of tension you are putting through the drive train by easing the effort you are putting on the pedals when shifting gear. Avoid changing to a larger gear than necessary, as this will burn excessive calories; the same is true of spinning in too small a gear. When pedaling into a climb, shift down through the gears one at a time. When the load through the legs has increased to a point where it is becoming more difficult to drive the pedals, change to an easier gear. Use momentum and try where possible to carry that free speed into the climb. Avoid using opposite extremes of large chainring and large sprocket on the rear, as this will wear the gears and put excessive strain on the chain.

When descending, shift up onto the big outer chainring, as this will remove the slack in the chain and put more tension into the rear derailleur; this will stop the chain slapping around and going into the spokes. This will also cover the teeth of the outer chainring, which could cause a nasty injury were you to have an accident where the bike fell on top of you.

Shoulders run parallel to the bars, and the skeletal system supports the body's mass.

SKILL 4: Track stands

Practicing track stands will help you to develop core stability and improve your balance. Building confidence at slow speed is key, as is practicing in a safe and controlled environment. This skill is useful when trail riding and often comes into play when taking on a technical climb. Use the following points in order to perfect your track stands:

- Find a slight uphill gradient with a good even surface. Pedal along in your middle chainring and about third gear on the rear, turning the cranks around very slowly. Avoid using the brakes; instead rely on tension and trail input.
- Feel the gradient working against you and slow your pedal rate right down so that you are barely moving.
- As your lead foot comes to the front, try and pause. (If you look at the cranks like a clock face, your drive-side crank will be at 2 o'clock if you lead with your right foot and at 10 o'clock if you lead with your left foot.)

- Simultaneously, turn your front wheel into the direction of your lead foot to about 45 degrees. The shoulders should be parallel to the handlebars, and remember that the wrists and heels should also be dipped.

> ▶▶ **Tip**
>
> Look for a small edge to rest your front wheel against. This will help you to focus on the trail surface and will provide extra resistance when you balance.

- Pause for longer each time and stay balanced on the spot.
- Move the bike in the lateral plane (left/right) by applying pressure through your hands and rocking the bike, moving the handlebars as opposed to turning (steering) the front wheel. Pressure, tension and resistance are key things to get to grips with in order to perfect this exercise.
- Keep focused on a spot about 3 ft in front of your wheel, relaxing the neck to look forward and downward. Stand tall over the bike so that the skeletal system (think of a tightrope walker) supports the body's mass rather than the muscular system.
- Turn the cranks around slowly through 360 degrees, feeling the tension in the legs, and pause again.
- Repeat the process, trying to pause for longer each time you stop.
- Avoid snapping on the cranks by back pedaling. We need to develop a super smooth pedal stroke using tension, and torque equals traction. Slow-speed riding is a great way to develop this skills set.

Progressing the technique

- Swap out your lead foot and try slowing to a stop with your trailing foot at the front. When we lead with our non-favored foot, we call this 'switch stance'. I am a firm believer that we should be able to ride with either foot leading. This way you will never be caught out when dealing with trail features.
- Try and hold the track stand for longer and longer.
- Challenge yourself by looking all around while doing your track stands, by engaging in a conversation or balancing with one hand.

SKILL 5: Looking – where we look, we go

From a standing start, you can focus on a spot just in front of your wheel, and look progressively further ahead as you get faster. The aim is ultimately to concentrate on the trail as far ahead as you can see at any given time. Avoid looking down immediately in front of you, especially when traveling at high speeds. Focus ahead on where you want to be on the trail – if you visualize yourself riding that line, you will.

But it's not simply a case of looking at any one spot at any given speed. We need to train our eyes so that they are capable of tuning in to fine detail, as well as taking in information using our peripheral vision.

For example, on slow climbs we need to look at the detail of the trail, taking into consideration the need for traction and focusing on finding the smoothest line that offers the most amount of grip. But at the same time we have to preempt and scan the trail ahead. We use our peripheral vision to keep an eye on the hill, looking for obstacles or changes in gradient that may require an adjustment in technique. You may spot in the distance something like a tight switchback, a continuation of the gradient or a technical obstacle.

The technique is the same when traveling on the flat or descending – it's just a simple case of having to respond faster. When you first start out, ride slowly then build up speed, giving yourself time to become accustomed to looking ahead and scanning the trail.

Getting to know a trail is imperative; that is not to say we should hone our skills to ride one trail alone, but that we need to develop our skills and technique so as to ride unseen trails with ease through our familiarity with certain features and shapes. To do this, we need to practice so that we respond instinctively – when we think about our movement instead of just doing it as a reaction, it takes that little bit longer to respond. The miniscule amount of time that passes while our brain thinks before sending messages to our muscles, that split second, is all it takes for a rock or root to take us out. Take a basic section of trail and we can highlight

There are many things on the trailside to distract you from your line – stay focused!

many features to be negotiated, primarily roots, rocks and earth (RRE) – there may be other factors to consider, but for now let's keep it to these three. All we need to do, and simple as it may sound, is to select our 2-inch-wide strip and commit to it. Staying relaxed, focused and using the correct technique, body position, footwork, pressure control and speed control, we can ride the most technically demanding trails with confidence.

SKILL 6: Footwork – pressure control

Cornering

Vision, speed control, body position, pressure control and footwork are the key components to mastering corners. We have to control our speed, preferably in a straight line rather than using the brakes mid-turn (this may cause us to slide out). Torque equals traction, so if we can pedal through a corner, or at least on the exit, we can corner faster and safer. A handy little phrase to remember is 'slow in – quick out'.

▶▶ Roots, rocks and earth (RRE)

The trail will sit raised from the ground around you, or be at the same level as the surrounding terrain, or be in a dip (referred to as a rut). Depending on the area, but almost inevitably, you will encounter one or more of the following (both on the trail ride line and at the side of the trail):

- Roots and tree stumps
- Rocks and boulders
- Earth

Developing your pedal timing, and so lining the pedal and crank arms up, will help you to avoid hitting RRE.

Slow-speed corner
- You will find that when climbing, there is no option but to pedal through the turn. On the odd occasion where there may be RRE that you have to negotiate, simply adapt your footwork accordingly to avoid smashing the pedals into the earth.
- As you approach the turn, look for the smoothest line and look through the turn to your exit.
- Simultaneously, pre-select your gear accordingly.
- Stay focused on your chosen exit point of the turn, looking through the corner.
- Steer around the turn and continue to look through the turn, pushing on the outer part of the handlebar rather than pulling (to increase your traction by pushing the tires into the ground).

▶▶ Tip

Remember that at higher speeds, you need to lean the bike to make it turn rather than using the handlebars!

Flat corners
For optimum cornering, you should ride into a turn with your footwork as follows:
- Right turn = left foot forward on the approach.
- Left turn = right foot forward on the approach.

When we stand up on the pedals, our hips are offset: they angle into or away from the corner, depending on which foot leads and what direction the trail takes. By using either the regular or switch stance, we can angle our body in the desired route of travel no matter which direction the turn takes. Try standing with feet shoulder-width apart and looking over either shoulder. Now stand with your feet offset, as if you are on your bike, and repeat the process. You should find that you can look farther over one shoulder than the other; this is why some of us have a preferred way of turning.

For a flat corner, ride into the initial part of the turn with crank arms level and the correct foot leading. Lean the bike into the turn, then start to lower the outer pedal by rolling the cranks around (it is important to have the correct gear selected so that there is an element of tension in the drive system).

You should aim to have your outer pedal down when you are about two-thirds through the corner. By developing this style and getting the timing correct, you can corner faster, harder and

Get your footwork dialed to the correct position on the approach and look through the turn.

Roll the cranks around as you progress through the turn.

safer. The process of holding the cranks level for longer can help when the bike loses traction – at this point, lowering the outer pedal increases dramatically the load going into the ground (think about standing on your bathroom scale and squatting down fast to make the needle bounce up). This will help the tire cut into the trail. To increase the grip even further, you can roll your foot inside your shoe – imagine you are putting a ski on its edge in order to turn. We can influence the bike's movement a huge amount with foot rolling (pressure control).

Should your wheel start to slide, try not to worry, as it will eventually find something to grip on again; even the smallest lip will offer support, if only for an instant. However, if you are carrying too much speed then you may continue to slide out.

As the outer crank reaches the bottom of the stroke, continue to turn the pedals and power out of the turn.

▶▶ How to corner a shallow radius left turn

- Approach the turn in your neutral stance with your right foot forward.
- Look through the corner for RRE.
- Select your line.
- Adjust your speed accordingly.
- Spot your exit.
- Lean the bike into the turn, keeping your torso vertical and your wrists and heels dipped.
- Keep your head still while remaining relaxed in the neck and shoulders.
- Stay focused on your exit point, hit it and ride out clean.

Progressing the technique
- Mark out a slalom course on a mellow gradient in a safe location.
- Ride the turns again and again, focusing on rolling the cranks around and having your outer foot down at the apex of each turn.
- Tighten up the course and change the slalom markers around so that each turn requires a different approach.

▶▶ How to corner medium and tight radius right turns

- Approach the turn with your left foot forward (switch stance, if your right foot is your favored foot).
- Look through the corner for RRE.
- Select your line.
- Adjust your speed accordingly.
- Spot your exit and stay focused.
- Lean the bike into the turn, keeping your torso vertical and your wrists and heels dipped.
- Keep your head still while remaining relaxed in the neck and shoulders.
- As you progress through the turn, slowly roll the cranks around – you are aiming to have your outer (left) foot down (so that the left crank at 6 o'clock) approximately two-thirds of the way through the turn.
- Continue with the smooth pedal stroke, and drive the cranks around as you exit the turn.

Bermed (banked) turns
- Apply the same technique that is used for flat corners. On bermed turns with a shallow radius you will be able to ride the section with your cranks level. Try and set up your footwork for the tighter turns in a sequence of corners.
- Momentum is your friend! Commit to the turn in order to stick to the trail; ride too slow and you will slip toward the bottom of the banking.
- Try and choose the smoothest line around the turn, setting your course when entering the berm.
- Avoid riding at the top of the berm, as it may be eroded ('blown out') farther around.
- Avoid riding on the loose material (scree) farther down on the inside of the turn.
- Try not to drop your inner elbow, as this will make the bike's front wheel tuck underneath you.
- Spot your exit, stay focused, and ride out clean.

We can also roll the crank around in bermed turns in order to gain more grip. As you reach the deepest point of the turn: drop your outer foot and roll the foot in the shoe; continue in one smooth action to drive the cranks around as you begin to exit the turn; spot your exit; and pedal out of the corner.

Notes from the trail

Throughout the process of developing a syllabus for mountain bike instruction, I experimented with many things. Different bikes, tires, suspension set-ups, handlebar widths and so on. The industry was constantly changing frame geometry and suspension travel, but I soon discovered that the core principles used to ride safely and smoothly were the same: look ahead, monitor your speed, dip the wrists, dip the heels, breathe and relax. However, a rider must change his or her style as necessary when riding different types of bikes.

SKILLS & TECHNIQUE

SKILL 7: Off camber and off-camber turns

When riding steep gradients on natural terrain you may come across off-camber sections (for example, when a trail is on an angle traversing a hillside there is nothing offering support, and the bike wants to slip out from underneath you), and there will probably be a corner or two thrown in for good measure as you traverse a hillside. Here are some pointers to help you deal with such sections:

- Look for supporting edges or a worn line to cross the hill and spot for RRE to support you (even a 0.5-inch lip would suffice).
- Increase the load through the pedals and, if the terrain is very steep, position your cranks so that the pedal on the downside is at the bottom (this will help with ground clearance and allow you to lean farther into the hill).
- Control your speed as you approach turns – your entry speed will need to be low, as the gradient you are dropping into will add pace.
- Try riding high and wide when going into turns.
- Spot your exit and stay focused.
- Lean the bike into the turn, keeping your torso vertical and your wrists and heels dipped.
- Keep the head still but remain relaxed.
- Look for lips to support you on the exit, and ride out clean.

Use more pressure through the feet when riding off camber.

SKILL 8: Wheelies

There are two ways to pick up the front end of the bike. The first method we will look at requires synchronizing a pedal stroke with scooping under the handlebars; the second method is the manual (see page 84).

A wheelie is used when taking a drop at super-slow speed or clearing a trail feature like a step when climbing. Timing is key here. You will find that pedaling provides most of the uplift, rather than pulling on the handlebars. Focus on scooping from underneath the bars and you'll find that you get more lift with less effort. By performing and perfecting proper wheelies we get used to the neutral balance point on the rear wheel and hopefully eliminate the fear of falling off the back ('looping out').

▶▶ Tip

I highly recommend using flat pedals instead of clip-in pedals. You will be able to step clear from the bike if it all gets a little too much!

- Find a slight uphill gradient on a smooth surface, with lots of space around you (short grass is the preferred choice, thanks to its forgiving nature).
- Select a low gear but stay in your middle chainring.
- Pedal along at a steady walking pace.
- Cover the rear brake. You may want to drag the brake slightly – balance brake tension against pedal tension. You can blend more brake in to prevent looping out should you lift beyond the neutral pivot point.
- As your lead foot comes around to 12 o'clock, dip your torso forward while pivoting through the hips and bending at the elbows.
- Just as the crank passes 1 o'clock (for right-foot lead, or 11 o'clock for left-foot lead), dynamically increase the load/pedal rate while simultaneously scooping under the bar and moving your torso backward, pivoting from the hips.
- As the torso moves back, extend your arms and lock out at the elbow (a move known as the 'pop and lock').

- Keep your rear end planted in the seat and imagine you are trying to drive the rear wheel underneath you. Also, it helps to keep your chin up a little.
- This is all done in one smooth fluid motion while continuing to pedal.

▶▶ Tip

If you feel you are going to loop out, lower your chest toward the stem or apply more rear brake.

If your wheelie drops off and you find that you are increasing your pedal rate and spinning through the gear, it means that you have not lifted the front wheel high enough with your initial scoop and pedal stroke.

SKILL 9: Pumping

Pumping is a key component to your riding CV. When we articulate our body in time with the motion of the bike and terrain, we flow through the trail in a seemingly effortless manner. When you are relaxed and supple, you can gain every ounce of momentum from the trail; if you tense up, stop breathing and dip the chin, you start to get out of rhythm with the trail. Once you have mastered feeling the trail and are moving in time you can add some effort on the downslopes and get that all-important free speed, which is the essence of pumping. The following pointers should help you to perfect this skill:

- Approach in your neutral stance.
- Keep the head still and focus through the feature.
- As the bike comes into the upslope, relax the arms at the elbows and let the handlebars come in closer to the torso.
- Remain vertical, keeping your head at the same height all the time, and use your limbs to absorb the impacts.
- When the front wheel crests the bump (or 'whoop'), you may need to use slight pressure – applied through your hands – to keep the front wheel on the dirt/ground.
- Now that the rear wheel is on the up, use your quads, flex the knees and bring the legs up into the torso.

- As the rear wheel crests the top of the whoop, extend your legs and use the power from your quads to drive the rear wheel down the far side of the feature.

SKILL 10: Manuals

Manuals do not rely on power – they are done while freewheeling on the descent. So although they look similar to wheelies, they are harder to master. I always like to make sure a rider knows how to wheelie first, using tension and pedaling to demonstrate core balance and power. Also the pump has to be mastered, as the subtle wrist and foot movements required help you develop a sense of timing over uneven ground.

Once a rider is confident with these skills, I take them freewheeling with wheels on the ground, feeling the shape of the trail and pumping. As an instinctive sense of timing develops, we move on to manuals.

By lifting our front wheel up, onto and over trail features, we eliminate a high percentage of resistance. Everything that opposes us, from small upslopes to square edges, can be manualed over. Getting the front center of the bike over a feature is key and will eliminate stalling. The following pointers should help you master this skill:

- Find a slight downhill gradient on a smooth surface, with lots of space around you (again, short grass is best).
- Roll along in neutral stance at a steady jogging pace, covering the rear brake to prevent looping out.

- Move forward, bending the elbows and pivoting through the hips – dip at the knee slightly as you do so and feel the pressure in the feet (you'll find that your toes are pointing down a bit at this stage).
- Dynamically flick your feet from toe-down to heel-down (this is where the majority of the lift comes from); by doing this you will naturally move backward toward the rear.
- Try to keep your hips running parallel to the trail, and avoid moving up or downward when you move toward the rear.
- As you flick your feet, simultaneously scoop under the bar and allow the arms to extend, ideally in one fluid motion.

▶▶ Tip

I cannot overemphasize how much difference it makes when you flick the heels down as you scoop under the bar – not only is the initial lift easier, but you can then hold the weight for longer. Also, lowering your seat can help you to sustain manuals for longer!

SKILL 11: The bunny hop

The bunny hop is a very useful tool, as it enables us to clear obstacles on the trail and pre-jump into downslopes. The correct technique involves lifting your two wheels independently and not simultaneously.

By lifting the front wheel using a manual then lifting ('hopping') the rear wheel over, we save energy and can move the bike left and right in the process. Our rear wheel only has to travel a short distance to clear the obstacle. To enable you to perform a lateral (sideways) hop, you will need to pivot on your rear wheel (see Skill 12 on page 88). Once again, it is important to learn good technique and I recommend that you use flat pedals while practicing. Here are some pointers:

- Find a slight downhill gradient on a smooth surface, with lots of space around you (short grass, if possible).
- Roll along in neutral stance at a steady jogging pace.
- Cover the rear brake to prevent looping out in case you lift beyond the neutral pivot point.
- Start the maneuver with the opening sequence of a manual (remember that the height of your hop will be defined by the height you can achieve in this initial lift).
- As the front wheel reaches its maximum height, lift the handlebars up and drive them up and away from you.
- Simultaneously spring up from your dipped heels. This is the snap point where you need to move in a fast, dynamic style. Your trailing foot will naturally point toe down, and you need

to pressure back against the pedal to help the lift.
- Lift your legs up into the torso, spot your landing and place the bike back down as gently as possible, with the rear wheel making contact just before the front.
- Ride out clean.

SKILL 12: The lateral bunny hop

To pull off a lateral bunny hop to the right, use the following pointers:

- As you roll into the maneuver, make a slight turn to the right – this should be done at the same time that you start the manual.
- As the manual reaches its peak height, turn slightly into the left as you make the snap and lift the rear wheel.

- Kick your feet across to the right – your left leg should be kicked across in an upward scooping motion.
- Place the bike back down gently with the rear wheel contacting just before the front.
- Ride out clean.

Practice by using your non-favored foot to start the hop – making it a 'switch bunny hop'. This is a great skill to perfect, as you never know when and where you're going to need it!

SKILL 13: Dealing with drop offs

Like all trail features, there are many different types of drop offs to encounter. Fortunately, you will only need to adjust your core technique slightly to conquer anything from a curb to a monster NorthShore drop off! As with all the skills listed previously, start small and build your confidence, then gradually gain height and distance.

Speed control is key here – mastering the ability to control your pace so that it suits the angles and distances will come with time. This is where repeatedly riding a trail feature will pay dividends.

Before attempting any drop off, you should first take a good look at its approach, the drop and the run out – otherwise known as 'entry, section, exit (ESE)'. Be sensible and choose a safe place to practice. Be aware of other trail users and, if in an urban environment, obey the rules of the road and look out for pedestrians and other road users.

SKILLS & TECHNIQUE

▶▶ Tip

Try and match the angle of your bike's landing with the gradient when landing into downslopes.

Slow-speed drop off

Where a drop off has a tight entry and exit, you will need to perform a slow-speed drop. Trail conditions, the gradient and RRE will also be factors to take into consideration and could force you into a slow-speed drop. The following pointers should help:

- Approach in your neutral position, spotting the lip and exit line.
- Adjust your speed and footwork accordingly.
- Perform a wheelie, just as your front wheel arrives at the lip.
- Ride over and off the lip, preferably coasting rather than pedaling – you may need to pedal through the lip with the rear wheel driving you forward to clear RRE, depending on your speed.
- Land rear wheel first, covering the rear brake, and absorb the landing through the legs.
- Once the rear wheel is touching the ground, control the front wheel and land it where required.
- Absorb the front wheel impact through the upper body – you will have to work harder on larger drops to keep the head still and ensure you don't hit the stem/handlebars.
- Return to your neutral position and ride out clean.

Higher-speed drop offs

- Having looked at the ESE, take a suitably long run-up. You may want to add a little extra distance so that you can settle into your neutral position before the drop. Stay relaxed and focused on the lip, with your heels and wrists dipped.
- Approach the lip while coasting along in your neutral stance and spot for your landing.
- Float off the lip and punch the bike out in front of you, driving through from the wrists and scooping the bars from underneath (rather than pulling up on them). Your lead foot should be making the same shape, dipping at the heel and

driving through. While your trailing foot will remain level, your toe may dip a little.

- Return to center over the bike as you free fall.
- Land the bike by extending your limbs just before you touchdown.
- Absorb the landing through the limbs. Remain focused, with your head still looking at your exit line and into the next section.

▶▶ Tip

Play with dipping your heels and applying different pressure through the pedals to get different outcomes. Rolling your feet, moving the handlebars, and changing the shape of your arms will also influence the direction the bike takes.

SKILL 14: Jumps

The skill that most mountain bikers aspire to mastering when they start out is jumping. Mastering jumps changes the way you look at and ride trails forever, and it enables you to ride faster and have a whole load more fun in the process.

We need to have perfected the manual and the bunny hop in order to jump consistently – the shapes we make and the techniques used are exactly the same as those performed in the bunny hop. The bunny hop is the safe way to practice, as you will become familiar with controlling each wheel independently in take-off, flight and landing.

Man-made take-offs require little physical effort; we simply let momentum do the work for us and use small inputs through pressure control to manage the shapes that our body and bike makes. Speed control is key. The correct pace combined with lift from the take-off transition will send us on a harmonious flight path.

▶▶ Tip

Where a trail suddenly steepens ('fades away'), we can pre-jump into the downslope by popping a bunny hop before the lip. Avoid flat landings and under-jumping (and so coming up short on a feature) at all costs!

A jump has a transition (curve) that leads into the main jump face; the top edge is called the lip, which may be rounded in shape or more angular and sharper in its curve.

Structure of the jump

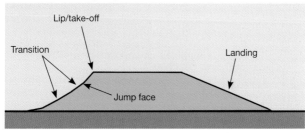

Small jumps (or what I refer to as 'bumps') have tight transitions that buck the bike when taken at speed. The short upslope does not allow for the full length (wheelbase) of the bike to sit on it, and the tight curve (transition) grabs the wheel and the bike gets stalled. You have to respond faster to deal with kicks from oversized bumps and badly built jumps when traveling at speed. If you move out of time with the trail, the outcome is often less than favorable.

Before taking on a jump, have a good look at it and consider its run-up, transition, take-off, landing and exit. Start small and work your way up to larger and longer jumps. BMX tracks are a great place to perfect jumping. The following pointers should help:

- Approach the feature/transition rolling along in your neutral stance, remaining focused on the lip and the landing zone.
- Control your speed well before you meet the transition.
- Time your opening manual moves as you flow through the start of the transition.

- Focus on the lip and think about going 'light at the lip'. This useful mantra helps you to naturally pump the take-off transition, because you're trying to be 'light'.
- Continue lifting the front end up, scooping under the bars as you exit the lip. Just before your rear wheel leaves the lip, you should be standing in the vertical position ready to lift the bike up into your torso.

- When fully airborne, spot your landing and lift the bike up into the torso with your legs – your arms should simultaneously extend up and out in front. When you hit larger jumps and have more air time, you can start to add a little flair!

- As you clear the lip on the far side, nose the bike down slightly to match the gradient of the downslope. If you were hitting a bump-type jump, you need to keep the bike level in order to match the lesser gradient.
- Your rear wheel should be fully over the lip and the bike matched to the angle of the landing/trail.

- Remain focused on your line, extend your arms and legs just before touchdown and then absorb the landing with your limbs.

Practice your technique

- To help build confidence and get a feel for the trail, roll up to the feature and manual out of the lip – try and go slow enough so that you stall, with your rear wheel pivoting on the lip. Remember, cover that rear brake!
- When the pace is just right, your front wheel should be exiting the take-off at the same angle (trajectory) as the jump face.

- Once you (a) have a good feeling of how the bike responds to the trail, (b) are timing your manual to near perfection and (c) have the bike exiting the jump face at the right trajectory, then place a stick (or other small object) just past the lip of the jump. Pick the pace up and bunny hop over the stick, land with both wheels simultaneously touching down and use your limbs to absorb the impact.

- Now repeat, but increase your pace and flow out of the lip. When the speed is matched to the shape and size of the jump, you should float over it with little effort and the lift will come naturally.

SKILL 15: Switchbacks

There are a huge variety of tight turns out there that 'switch back' on themselves. You will often find that the steeper the terrain, the tighter the switchback. The trail is usually narrower and so your speed will need to be adjusted accordingly.

Open switchbacks

- If it is not possible to ride the outside line due to RRE, approach as far over as the terrain will allow on the outside edge of the trail.
- Enter the switchback with your cranks level in the neutral stance. Remember to have your footwork perfected ('dialed') for maximum grip between the tire and trail surface. Keep your heels and wrists dipped, controlling the speed in a straight line and using as much front brake as possible. Stay relaxed and do your braking early.
- Try to avoid locking the rear wheel, as this will reduce your stopping power, erode the trail and cause braking bumps and ruts.
- Look down to the trail below, spotting for RRE and pre-selecting your exit line.
- Enter by swinging wide, using the bank where possible or riding as wide as the trail will allow. Carve up the bank while looking through the turn. If there is no bank to use, stay out wide and look through the turn to the trail horizon.
- Cut down off the bank, aiming for an apex about three-quarters of the way around the turn. When you hit the mid-point of the turn, drop your outer foot so that the cranks are in the vertical position. Continue to look through the turn, steering by pushing with your outer hand while pressing down through the pedals with dipped heels.
- Roll the cranks back to level in a fluid motion as you complete the last part of the turn. This will set you up for the next switch-back or simply allow you to pedal out of the turn.

▶▶ Tip

Remember to look for RRE to support you as you make the turn.

Tight switchbacks: Method 1

- Control your speed upon entry, as with the open switchback, spotting your exit line as you approach.
- Follow the same points as for the open switchback – look through for your exit, watch your footwork and speed control.
- Slow to a near stop, looking into the turn.
- Gently ease off the brakes and simultaneously move toward the back of the bike, toward the inside of the turn.
- Keep your cranks level (this is very important) and your heels dipped.
- Push through with your outer hand and continue looking through the turn.
- Avoid any RRE that could impede your momentum and try not to snatch at the brakes, as this will pitch you upward or skid the rear wheel.
- On super-tight, steep switchbacks, you will practically pivot on the rear wheel.
- As you exit the turn, return to your neutral stance for maximum braking efficiency. You may need to repeat the process for the next switchback.

Notes from the trail

1994 was an amazing year. I trained hard the winter before and qualified to compete in the World Championships. I took the trip of a lifetime to Vail and raced in the dual slalom and downhill. This was my first big mountain experience and the exposure to longer and more technically challenging trails changed my view forever. Exposure to a variety of terrain is imperative if you want to progress your riding.

Tight switchbacks: Method 2

To master this technique, you will first need to have perfected Skill 16: The nose wheelie (see page 104). When you have, the following pointers will help:

- Control your speed upon entry to the switchback, as in the previous section, but this time you will need a little extra momentum as you enter the turn. Spot your exit line as you approach.
- Spring up from your dipped heels and simultaneously apply more front brake while starting to turn in.
- Coast into the turn on your front wheel, kicking the rear end of the bike around with your feet (pushing across with the inside foot).
- When the bike is approximately 90 degrees to the turn, release the front brake slightly and roll down the gradient while still turning in and kicking the feet across.
- Push your feet down, planting the rear wheel, and roll out.

This method is much faster but does come with the associated risks of falling/injury. When encountering multiple corners, using both of these two techniques will mean that you have to re-adjust your footwork when exiting the turn in order to be set up for the next switch. Remember that you should always perfect your technique in a safe and controlled environment before putting your new-found skills into practice out on the trail.

Practice your technique

Find a slight downhill gradient. Place a cone or soft object on the ground and roll around it as slowly as you can. Work closer and closer to the object as you make tight turns around it. Aim to get your rear wheel touching the object as you make super-tight turns. Now repeat, riding it in the opposite direction.

SKILL 16: The nose wheelie

The nose wheelie (when the rear wheel is lifted in the air while the rider pivots around the front axle) is mainly used by trail riders, but mountain bikers benefit greatly by being familiar with the feeling of pivoting over the front axle. The skill can be very useful in tight technical terrain, as shown in the previous method for addressing switchbacks.

The ability to blend the front brake in smoothly is essential. As with all skills, you should practice this technique in a safe spot with good visibility and a 'friendly' surface. Use the following pointers:

- Roll along at walking pace in your neutral stance.
- Spot where you want to come to a stop.
- Feed the front brake in slowly while simultaneously popping up from your dipped heels.
- Lift the legs up into the torso to absorb the forward motion of the bike.
- Lower the bike back to the floor by extending the legs.

Progressing the technique
- Place a marker on the ground (use something like a plastic cone that will distort/move should you clip it).
- Try and make a turn around the marker in a nice smooth radius.
- Approach at different angles and ride imaginary lines around the marker.
- As you gain confidence try working on steeper gradients. Performing nose manuals down steeper banks will help build your confidence. Play with wheel placement by planting the rear wheel onto a marked spot, curb, etc.
- Try doing a nose wheelie with your non-favored foot leading (i.e., in switch stance).
- Try going around the marker in the opposite direction.
- Then try going around the marker in the opposite direction in switch stance.

Notes from the trail

I was an avid skateboarder in my childhood and heavily inspired by the attendant scene. The Zephyr skateboard team was a huge influence; they were masters at riding with style. I applied this concept of developing a style to my mountain biking and was soon spotted on the national race circuit as a rider to watch.

5 Bike set-up guide

Setting up the cockpit

Making subtle changes to bar width, stem length, stem height and brake lever position will have a dramatic effect on your body position and neutral stance. The result will give you either more or less control. When making changes to your set-up, it is a good idea to mark the position of a component where possible before making the change. This way, you have a reference point to compare with or refer back to should you not like the change. With all adjustments, start small.

Bar adjustments

Wider bars give greater control at higher speeds and lower your chest toward the stem, putting more weight over the front end and into the front wheel. They do however give a more clumsy ride at slower speeds in rough terrain. There will be a cut-off point that suits you, depending on the width of your shoulders. Bear in mind that wider bars will distribute the impact from bumps into different muscle groups in the arms and shoulders.

Riser bars will come in different sweeps (the angle that the bar curves toward you) and rises (the angle between the part that clamps into the stem and the part you hold). Adjustments to your ride position can be made by altering the angle that you clamp the bars onto the stem. As a rough guide, the riser section between the two curves should be in the vertical position when viewed from the side. The grip area should sweep upward and backward slightly.

Stem adjustments

The steering response on a shorter stem is faster; small inputs make a big change to the angle of the front wheel. A longer stem requires more movement to get the same result (bar width has the same effect). Longer stems make it harder to lift the front end and the majority of your mass is on the arms and is over the front-center of the bike. Shorter stems put you in a more up-right position, which helps keep the head up and makes it easier to lift the front wheel up, onto and over obstacles.

Stem height can be adjusted by moving the spacers on the steerer tube so that they sit below or above the clamp. You can also choose to run a stem with different degrees of rise. A 0-degree rise stem (i.e., flat) will help get weight over the front wheel whereas a higher-rise stem will reduce this and put you in a more upright riding position farther toward the rear half of the bike.

Lever and gear shifter position (inboard, outboard, angle and reach)

Your brake levers should be positioned so that you can rest your forefinger in the cup or hook shape at the end of the lever. This gives you maximum control, allowing you to apply the brake smoothly and steadily. The ideal angle of the lever has been under debate for some time, and I have to say that there is an element of personal preference to consider here. First we have to decide where we are over the bike when we set up the angle. As we use our brakes mostly when descending, it makes sense to be standing tall and proud over the bike in our neutral stance to make the adjustment. You should have your wrists dipped to push and drive the bike forward, and so the lever should be in the appropriate position.

Downhill riders run their brake levers much flatter in order to help with dipping the wrist and driving through. If you set the brake lever angle so it is 'in-line' with your forearm, as per the old way of doing things, there is more chance of your hand slipping forward off the bars when you take hits from the front, and of having less control over the brake lever when dipping the wrists to deal with rough ground.

Different combinations of gear shifter and brake lever make it easier or harder to get that nice sweet spot, where your levers are far enough in so that you can grab/squeeze the end of the blade and still reach your gear shifter. You might have to find a compromise here, but bear in mind that the importance of being able to slow down and control your speed safely outweighs being able to shift gears efficiently.

Move brake levers in for one-finger braking.

Further adjustments can be made to the brake lever in the form of reach. Most set-ups have a small hexagonal-head grub screw (i.e., a screw without a head) or a dial that moves the lever blade in toward the bar or out away. The reach should be adjusted so that you are not overstretching to reach the lever but also not so close that it hits the grip before the brake is fully on (you will find an element of sponginess to the end part of the lever travel).

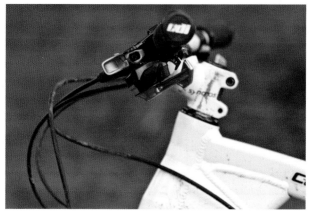

Bars should sweep back and up slightly.

Saddle adjustments (height, angle, fore, aft)

Start by setting your seat at the correct height for pedaling (if you ride freestyle street, free-ride dirt or downhill, this is not so important). Do this by sitting on your bike and leaning up against a wall with both feet on the pedals. Drop one pedal so that the cranks run in line with your seat tube, just off the vertical. Place the lower foot so that the heel is on the pedal; your leg should be nearly locked out; do not overstretch or hyperextend at the knee. This gives you a rough starting position from where you may wish to raise the post (and increase pedal efficiency) or lower it (to provide more clearance and stability) by a few millimeters.

Mountain biking done efficiently and effectively requires you to be out of the saddle and standing on the pedals for a considerable time, so running your seat low is no bad thing. However do not go to extremes, as you will open yourself up to the potential of knee damage and other muscular dysfunction. Downhill, free-riders and street riders will opt for running their seats much lower to assist with clearance; this allows the bike to move around more underneath them as they traverse large bumps. To perform certain skills, like the manual, it is better to have your seat lowered because you need to move the hips around in the area that your saddle would be when set at the height for normal riding.

Setting the seat's angle

Dropping the nose of the saddle can help relieve lower back ache and will remove pressure from sensitive areas. The starting point for all adjustments should be made with your seat running parallel to the ground, with your bike on a flat surface. See what suits you best, and avoid angles that are in the extremes.

Fore and aft adjustment

Slide the saddle forward and backward in the post on its rails. This adjustment will affect the path that your knee takes when pedaling. Remember that reach adjustment should be done by changing the stem and not by moving the saddle. To get the saddle in the correct position, you need to be sitting on your bike, leaning against a wall. Move the cranks so that they are level (parallel to the floor), and place the ball of your foot over the pedal

Some saddle rails will have markings on already, making for easy adjustment.

axle. Sight a line down from the center of the knee – this should run through the pedal axle.

Pedals and spring tension (for clip-in pedals)

Start with the spring tension at its weakest. If you are using good technique, you will not suffer from accidental unclipping and you can increase the tension as your confidence builds. Make sure that your cleats are tight and square, as loose cleats could twist and you will be stuck to the pedal. Badly aligned cleats could result in damage to the ankles, knees and hip joints.

First-aid kit contents

The kit
Always ride with a first-aid kit. Not just for you, but for other people you may meet on the trailside. But there is no point having the first-aid kit packed if you have no idea how to use its contents.

- Assorted dressings
- Antiseptic wipes
- Antiseptic cream
- Assorted bandages
- Triangle bandage

- Gloves
- Face shield resuscitator
- Microporous tape
- Safety pins
- Scissors

6 Emergency procedures

I have been in numerous scenarios where I have been lucky enough to be assisted by someone with first-aid training. I'm grateful beyond words for their level-headed approach to situations that easily could have become life threatening.

You may be one of the lucky few who never has a crash. You may never have to deal with another rider who departs from the trail and requires first aid or a fast ride to the hospital. But I still hope that the following information inspires you to sign up for a first-aid course – ideally one that covers emergency procedures in the outdoor environment.

Speed and/or gradient play a role in all accidents. The faster a rider is going, and the steeper the trail they are riding, the higher the chance of a more serious scenario. Though some slow-speed falls can result in serious injury, the rider would have to land very awkwardly. The surrounding terrain of course plays a role in the potential risk: if you are riding in an area with exposed rocks then there is obviously a higher risk than if you were riding on rolling grass hills.

Notes from the trail

I was practicing a challenging downhill section on a narrow, steep trail in my local woods. I tried to clear a set of stairs by drop jumping them rather than rolling down them, but my front wheel clipped a root on landing and I was sent flying into a tree. I can only remember small parts of the journey to the hospital, and I'm grateful to my friends for dealing with the situation in a cool, calm and collected manner. Had I been on my own, I might not be here today.

With a little initiative you can use the casualty's jersey, T-shirt, or jacket to make a sling.

So, if you come across an accident scene where it is likely that a rider was traveling at high speed, be prepared for the worst. Whether the rider has been thrown over the handlebars or been thrown off the side ('high-sided'), they are going to be lucky to get away without an injury. The worst possible scenario is that you find a person who is unconscious and not breathing; in this case, your first-aid training is invaluable, as you will need to give the casualty chest compressions and mouth-to-mouth resuscitation.

ACCIDENT PROCEDURE

STEP 1: Assess the situation

- Protect yourself: go back up the trail and block it, perhaps with your bike, to avoid a rider crashing into you both.
- Check out the terrain: make sure it's safe for you to approach (are they lying on a steep slope?) and try to piece together what happened.
- Observe the situation. How are they lying? Is their mouth covered? Look for signs of bleeding and obvious breakages.
- Talk to them – shout if necessary: if you get a verbal response or a movement, you know they are conscious and breathing, though they may be injured. Go to step 2.
- Touch them: pinch the ear or squeeze a shoulder. No response means you've got an unconscious casualty on your hands. **Go to page 118.**

- Look at the chest, does it rise and fall? Listen for their breath or place your hand or face near their mouth to feel for breath. Or try to take their pulse at the neck or wrists. **If they are not breathing, go to page 119.**

STEP 2: Getting help

- Don't be too shy to call for help. Simply shout, nice and loud, 'Help! Help! Help!' There may be someone nearby who can assist you.
- If the casualty responds vocally or with movement, leave them where they are and call the emergency services, then return to support them.
- If you don't have a phone signal and you are in a group, try if possible to keep two people with the casualty while two go for help.
- If you are alone and don't have a mobile signal, you will need to go yourself. Make sure you know exactly where you leave the injured person. Mark the trail, if necessary. Stay calm as you go – you don't want to risk an injury. Leave the casualty as safe and comfortable as possible while they wait.
- **Go to step 3.**

The recovery position

Upper leg across the body to place knee on the ground

Lie them on their side

Lower arm out away from the body

Upper arm across the body, place palm-down on the ground

STEP 3: Waiting for help

- Whether they are being left alone or with someone, put the casualty in the recovery position. They are likely to be on uneven ground, so don't try too hard – just ensure that the airway is clear so that nothing can block the mouth or nose.
- If you suspect a head/neck injury, use your common sense and try to get them in a position that will keep the airway clear without moving them excessively.
- Check the body over for other injuries and attend to them to the best of your ability, stopping large bleeds and supporting potential breakages and fractures.
- Talk to them, keeping them alert and focused on you.
- Use your spare clothes to help keep their core temperature up while help is sought.
- If you have called for help or sent a friend, check for continued breathing and monitor the casualty's pulse every 3–5 minutes. Keep a note of these and inform the emergency services.

✚ Moving the casualty

Remember: if possible you should never move a casualty; only move them if thay are in immediate danger where they are and there is no other viable option. You may need to move them to a safer place, though if there is any evidence of a head or neck injury, do so by providing careful support and only if you think there is no option. Take your time and make sure you support the head throughout the process. This is a tough call for any first responder, but if there is further risk to you and the casualty, then it has to be done.

Support the head when moving the casualty

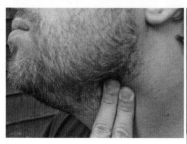 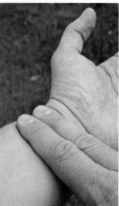

To locate the pulse on the neck, press your finger in the soft area next to the Adam's apple. For the wrist, face the casualty's palm upward and place two fingers on the inside of the wrist at the base of the thumb.

If the casualty is not conscious

✚ **In this situation, it can save lives to know what you are doing. This book is no substitute for a first-aid course.**

- Check the airway: tilt the head while lifting the chin (see photo A). Remove any blockage and check for breathing.
- If there is the potential for head/neck injury, then use a chin lift with a jaw thrust to clear the airway: lift the jaw away from the skull while keeping the head tilted but as still as possible (see photo B). Look for signs of breathing.
- Take 10 seconds to decide if they are breathing or not.
- If breathing, **go to step 2, page 115.** If not, **go to page 119.**

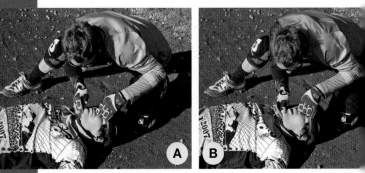

✚ **Learn your ABCs**

A = airway: is there a clear passage? If not, clear it.
B = breathing: are they?
C = circulation: can you feel a pulse, or see or hear them breathe?

If the casualty is not breathing

If you are with friends, someone will call or fetch help for you. If not, make sure the airway is clear and will remain clear while you go for help. When you return move straight into the sequence below – every second counts.

Begin with chest compressions
- First, turn the casualty onto their back.
- Place one hand in the center of the chest, just below where the two halves of the ribcage meet (so not the ribs, and not the abdomen).
- Put your other hand on top and interlock your fingers.
- Kneel upright and, keeping your arms straight and using the heel of your hand, compress the chest to a depth of 1.5–2 in.
- Release the pressure after each compression.
- Repeat this 30 times in quick succession, counting aloud if that helps you. Do not worry about damaging the ribs: your priority now is to preserve their life.

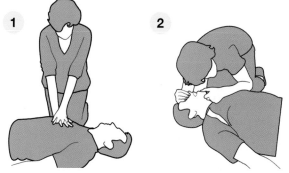

Move on to CPR, or rescue breaths
- After 30 compressions, give two rescue breaths.
- Ensure that the airways are open, so maintain the head tilt.
- Place one hand on the casualty's chin and **pinch their nostrils shut** with the finger and thumb of the other hand.
- Fill your lungs with air and place your lips around their mouth. Try to create a good seal. Using a face mask is recommended if you are carrying one in your first-aid kit.

- Blow into their mouth until the chest lifts – this should take 2–3 seconds. Move your head away to see if the chest falls. If it does, the breath was effective.
- Give a second breath, making sure that the head is still tilted correctly.
- Continue the sequence of 30 chest compressions followed by two rescue breaths.
- If you cannot get a good seal and the chest does not rise, check again that the airway is clear, and ensure that you have an adequate head tilt and chin lift before trying again.

Carry on with this sequence of chest compression and CPR

- Every minute, stop and check for signs of life (slight breathing or coughing, any physical movement). Take no longer than 10 seconds over this assessment.
- If you are confident that circulation is present (i.e., the casualty is breathing, opening their eyes or you can feel a pulse within 10 seconds), continue with rescue breathing if necessary or until the casualty starts breathing on their own.
- If breathing returns but the casualty remains unconscious, position them in the recovery position and monitor their condition, as you may need to start the rescue breath process again.
- If there is another person with you who is first-aid trained, then change over every two minutes to avoid fatigue.
- If you are unable or unwilling to give rescue breaths, then give compressions only.
- Continue resuscitation until qualified help arrives, until the casualty starts breathing normally, or until you become exhausted.

Hopefully you will never have to deal with a casualty who is not breathing. You are more likely to come across a rider who has perhaps broken a bone or lost some skin, and in certain circumstances breakages and fractures can be life threatening. Large arteries could be ruptured, causing massive bleeding either internally or externally, or a rib may have punctured a lung. Some very innocuous-looking accidents could have dire consequences, so always check to see if someone is OK following a fall.

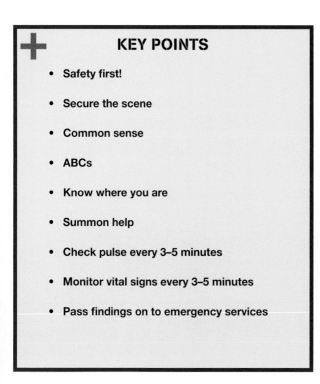

KEY POINTS

- **Safety first!**

- **Secure the scene**

- **Common sense**

- **ABCs**

- **Know where you are**

- **Summon help**

- **Check pulse every 3–5 minutes**

- **Monitor vital signs every 3–5 minutes**

- **Pass findings on to emergency services**

This chapter alone could fill a whole book – I really do recommend that you get online and sign up for a course; you could make the difference for some unlucky soul. There have been a few occasions where my training has come into play: some on the trail and others in situations where members of the public have failed to respond to the needs of a fellow human being. You will not regret spending the money and doing the training.

GLOSSARY

Air When a rider leaves the ground following a drop or jump, they are 'catching air'.

Barrel adjuster Small dial that threads into the shifters and/or derailleur, allowing cable tension to be fine-tuned.

Bead The part of the tire that locks into the lip of the wheel rim.

Bermed Banked turn.

Bio-mechanical slang for physical injury.

Blow through When a bike uses all of its suspension travel, it 'blows through'.

Bolt-through The system which attaches a wheel with a hollow axle to either the frame or fork.

Bottom out To hit the bump stop (end of the available travel) on your suspension unit.

Braze-on An additional mounting point that is welded to a frame (including cable guides).

Buzz The response from the trail that is felt through the bike, created by lots of small bumps close together.

Cassette The cluster of cogs/sprockets that bolts onto the free-hub body on the rear hub.

Chainring Front drive ring connected to the crank arm spider (a section on the drive-side crank arm).

Coasting Rolling along without pedaling.

Compression The force exerted on you and your suspension.

Cranks The arms that the pedals and chainrings connect to.

Derailleur The rear mechanism that the chain runs through, enabling you to change gear.

Dialed Rider slang for perfected.

Dish The offset (position to the left or right of center) of the hub once it's laced with spokes and attached to the wheel rim.

Downhill Where the trail descends.

Drop off A trail feature that is too steep to ride down, so you 'drop off' it.

ESE Stands for 'entry/section/exit'.

Fast patch An adhesive patch for fixing a punctured inner tube.

Free-ride dirt Riding timber and dirt jumps.

Freestyle street Riding in urban areas doing tricks.

Front fork The part of the frame set that holds the front wheel.
Full suss Slang for 'full suspension'.

Headset The component parts that allow the fork to fit and turn in the head tube of the main frame.
High frequency Fast, close movement of the trail.

IMBA International Mountain Biking Association.
Indexed Marked points where a gear is selected on a thumb shifter.

Kevlar tires The tire bead is fabricated from Kevlar strands.
Knobby Terminology that describes the blocks of rubber on a tire.

Lip The edge or launch point from a jump or drop.

Mechanicals A mechanical failure.
Multi-tool Compact tool which includes Allen keys, Torx head keys, screwdrivers and a chain-breaking tool.

Neutral stance (or position) The standing riding position while coasting.
Nose wheelie A skill where you put the bike up onto the front wheel.
NS Abbreviation for 'NorthShore' – raised wooden trails/platforms of varying widths.

Play Another term for movement.
Presta Tall, narrow valve with a locking top nut.

Quick link Chain-joining link (a permanent method of joining a chain).

Race Shaped metal ring, component part that the bearing sits against.
Rapid rise A gear system where the spring in the rear derailleur is reversed; the shifters work in reverse order compared to a regular system.
Rebound The force that returns your suspension unit to its nominal position.
RRE Stands for 'roots/rocks/earth'.
Rut A deep groove in the trail surface.

Sag/droop The amount of pre-load you have on your suspension unit.
Satphone Abbreviation for satellite telephone.
Shimano Japanese component manufacturer.
Shock Abbreviation for shock absorber.

Slick A tire with minimal or no tread.

Spoke key Tool for adjusting the spoke nipple.

SRAM American bicycle component manufacturer.

Stanchion The inner tube on a suspension fork, also called slider.

Switchback A very tight radius turn where the trail switches back on itself.

Topographic A very highly detailed map.

Track stand A skill where you balance your bike on the spot.

True Straight.

Visual cues/trail input Trail features, including RRE, to respond to or perform on/off.

Wash out To slide out, lose control.

Wheelie A skill where you ride along with your front wheel in the air.

RESOURCES

www.bikeradar.com	News and features on all aspects of biking
www.dirt.mpora.com	Cycling magazine for downhill riders
www.imba.com	International Mountain Biking Association
www.mtbskills.co.uk	The author's mountain bike training academy
www.omnimap.com	Maps
www.singletrackworld.com	Online cycling magazine, predominantly for cross-country trail riders
www.uci.ch	The global governing body for cycling

The Mountain Bike Skills Manual, Clive Forth
The in-depth guide to mountain biking; contains warm-up
information and exercises for getting the most out of your riding.

INDEX